Enhancing Microsoft Content Management Server with ASP.NET 2.0

ASP.NET 2.0 Master Pages, Themes, Site Navigation, and the Membership Provider Model in Microsoft Content Management Server Development

Use the powerful new features of ASP.NET 2.0 with your MCMS Websites

Spencer Harbar

Lim Mei Ying

Stefan Goßner

BIRMINGHAM - MUMBAI

Enhancing Microsoft Content Management Server with ASP.NET 2.0

ASP.NET 2.0 Master Pages, Themes, Site Navigation, and the Membership Provider Model in Microsoft Content Management Server Development

First published: July 2006

Production Reference: 1180706

Published by Packt Publishing Ltd.
32 Lincoln Road
Olton
Birmingham, B27 6PA, UK.

ISBN 1-904811-52-3

www.packtpub.com

Cover Image by www.visionwt.com

Credits

Authors

Spencer Harbar

Lim Mei Ying

Stefan Goßner

Reviewers

Andreas Klein

Mick Badran

Chester Ragel

Joel Ward

Development Editor

Douglas Paterson

Technical Editor

Niranjan Jahagirdar

Editorial Manager

Dipali Chittar

Indexer

Mithil Kulkarni

Proofreader

Chris Smith

Production Coordinator

Manjiri Nadkarni

Layouts and Illustrations

Shantanu Zagade

Cover Designer

Shantanu Zagade

About the Authors

Spencer Harbar, an MCSD for Microsoft .NET, MCSE and MVP for MCMS, has over twelve years commercial experience of architecture, design, development, deployment, and operational support of web-based applications and hosting platforms for some of Europe's largest organisations.

Spencer maintains www.mcmsfaq.com: an MCMS resources portal, and is active in the public newsgroups. His experience of MCMS goes back to the days of NCompass Resolution, and he has been involved in many enterprise implementations.

Currently working as an independent consultant, Spencer delivers enterprise content management and portal systems architecture, design, development, and deployment solutions, application security best practices, threat modeling, and the implementation of highly available Windows-Server-System-based hosting platforms.

Product expertise includes MCMS, SharePoint Technologies, IIS, SQL Server, Commerce Server and BizTalk Server, Windows Security, PKI, and High Availability.

Selected clients include Barclays Bank, Scottish Power plc, HBOS, Microsoft, The Royal Bank of Scotland, Scottish Enterprise, Centrica, Clifford Chance, The Automobile Association, and BASF.

Spencer resides in Edinburgh, UK.

Lim Mei Ying is a Senior Consultant with Avanade and has extensive experience in setting up MCMS systems at the enterprise level. She has spent many hours figuring out the dos and don'ts of the product, and enjoys finding new ways to solve MCMS-related problems.

She contributes actively to the newsgroup community and is a Microsoft Most Valuable Professional for Content Management Server. Mei Ying lives on the sunny island of Singapore and blogs at `http://meiyinglim.blogspot.com`. She also co-authored the earlier book, *Building Websites with Microsoft Content Management Server* (ISBN 1-904811-16-7, Packt Publishing).

Thanks to my husband, Louis, for the much needed support throughout the many months of writing. Special thanks to my family and friends for their encouragement.

Stefan Goßner works for Microsoft as an Escalation Engineer in the Developer Support department. He provides customers with technical solutions to problems related to Microsoft Internet Server Products. Stefan has a wide understanding of all areas of MCMS.

His contributions to the newsgroup have helped many people to implement MCMS solutions in corporations around the globe to the point where it has been said that if you don't know Stefan, then you're probably new to MCMS.

Stefan maintains a huge MCMS 2002 FAQ on the Microsoft website, and provides MCMS tips and tricks on his personal blog `http://blogs.technet.com/stefan_gossner`.

Stefan has also written the books *Building Websites With Microsoft Content Management Server* (ISBN 1-904811-16-7, Packt Publishing), and *Advanced Microsoft Content Management Server Development* (ISBN 1-904811-53-1, Packt Publishing).

He lives in Munich, Germany, and can be reached at `webmaster@stefan-gossner.de`

I would like to thank my girlfriend Michaela, for her support throughout months of writing, reviewing, and coding for the book. Also many thanks to my friends in the MCMS Support Teams worldwide and to my friends in the MCMS product team in the US.

About the Reviewers

Andreas Klein started in the PC business in 1981, working as a consultant for several years before joining Microsoft in 1990. Since then he has held programming trainings. On the technical side, he has covered many different areas, including Win16 (Windows 2.x, 3.x) and Win32 Application and Driver Programming, helping customers manage their systems running Windows 9x, Windows NT, and later versions, and even Exchange 4.0 - 2000.

His current focus is web server scenarios (IIS, MCMS 2002), DHTML programming, and PKI/Security concepts in the IT scope.

Mick Badran has been performing Microsoft technical classroom-based training for more than nine years, and has over 12 years commercial development experience in various languages. Mick has been consulting for Microsoft in areas of CMS, SPS, and BizTalk for over five years. He also specializes in customized training in these areas.

Mick speaks at various Microsoft Events such as TechEd and Security summits, and is a BizTalk MVP.

He can be reached at mickb@breezetraining.com.au, and would love to hear your feedback.

Joel Ward works as a web developer and technical manager. Once destined to be an architect, he switched tracks midway through college and instead graduated with a degree in Integrative Arts from the Pennsylvania State University. His professional career has taken him on a journey through design, programming, usability, and accessibility.

Joel has enjoyed working with MCMS since its first release in 2001. Over the years, Joel has been active in the newsgroups and has been recognized as a Microsoft Most Valuable Professional for his work in the MCMS community.

He enjoys a good challenge, which includes working on projects that use ASP.NET, MCMS, and SharePoint.

Joel lives in the Commonwealth of Virginia in the United States. You can visit his website at http://www.wardworks.com/joel/.

Table of Contents

Preface

Enhancing Microsoft Content Management Server with ASP.NET 2.0 delves into the integration of key ASP.NET 2.0 features such as Master Pages, Site Navigation, Themes and Skins, and the Membership Provider Model with Microsoft Content Management Server 2002 (MCMS) Service Pack 2.

Each chapter builds upon the last, walking through these new features available to MCMS developers and building a sample site similar to that presented in our previous book, *Building Websites with Microsoft Content Management Server* from Packt Publishing January 2005 (ISBN 1-904811-16-7).

What This Book Covers

Chapter 1 walks you through the installation and configuration of MCMS 2002 Service Pack 2 (SP2), along with SQL Server 2005 and Visual Studio 2005 on a single developer workstation. There are two approaches to setting up a development environment for SP2: an upgrade from a previous SP1a installation or starting from scratch and building a fresh installation including SP2. We will cover both approaches in this chapter.

In *Chapter 2* we spend some time getting familiar with the MCMS Service Pack 2 development environment, which is slightly different from what we are used to with previous versions of MCMS and Visual Studio. We will cover these changes and a number of tips for working within the SP2 development environment, such as the creation of custom MCMS Visual Studio 2005 templates.

Chapter 3 introduces you to one of the best new features introduced with ASP.NET 2.0, master pages, which allow developers to enforce common layout and behavior across pages within an application. While at first pass many master pages concepts are similar to those of MCMS templates, there are a number of benefits to be gained by taking advantage of master pages within MCMS applications. This chapter provides an overview of the benefits of using master pages and a step-by-step guide for implementing them in your MCMS applications, where they become master templates!

Chapter 4 covers the new ASP.NET 2.0 Navigation provider model and controls, and how to integrate them into your MCMS applications. Developing site navigation controls is an exercise that often leaves developers in a dilemma. Early versions of Visual Studio did not provide any ready-to-use navigation controls. Developers had to choose between spending many hours building controls from scratch or expand project budgets to purchase shrink-wrapped software.

In *Chapter 5* we will see how a common look and feel can be applied efficiently to an MCMS site by using themes. We will create skins and cascading style sheets and demonstrate how they work together to define the appearance of a site. Finally, we will discuss an essential customization required for themes to work correctly in an MCMS site.

Chapter 6 covers the Membership Provider Model, one of the key new concepts introduced with ASP.NET 2.0, which makes it significantly easier to develop web applications that utilize third-party or custom membership stores. In addition ASP.NET 2.0 ships with a number of authentication controls related to role membership, which vastly reduce the amount of code required to implement forms authentication and associated functionality in your applications. This chapter shows how to use these features to improve the implementation of Forms Authentication and provides a more elegant solution for "account mapping" scenarios whereby authentication takes place against an external store and the accounts are mapped to Windows accounts for the purposes of MCMS authorization.

In *Chapter 7* we present a number of tips along with code samples for working with ASP.NET 2.0 and MCMS SP2, and offer implementation advice for those considering migration to the upcoming Microsoft Office SharePoint Server 2007.

What You Need for This Book

This book has been written for MCMS developers who are comfortable with the material presented in our previous book, *Building Websites with Microsoft Content Management Server*, and have a solid grasp of C#. To use this book you need to have access to the following:

- Visual Studio 2005 (any edition).
- Microsoft Content Management Server 2002 Service Pack 2 (any edition). A 120 day evaluation of MCMS is available from http://www.microsoft.com/cmserver.

We walk through the various pre-requisites for installation in Chapter 1. All examples presented use Microsoft Windows XP Professional Service Pack 2.

Conventions

In this book, you will find a number of styles of text that distinguish between different kinds of information. Here are some examples of these styles, and an explanation of their meaning.

There are three styles for code. Code words in text are shown as follows: "We can include other contexts through the use of the `include` directive."

A block of code will be set as follows:

```
public string FirstName
{
    get
    {
        return txtFirstName.Text.Trim();
    }
}

// Last Name
public string LastName
{
    get
    {
        return txtLastName.Text.Trim();
    }
}
```

When we wish to draw your attention to a particular part of a code block, the relevant lines or items will be made bold:

```
public string FirstName
{
    get
    {
        return txtFirstName.Text.Trim();
    }
}

// Last Name
public string LastName
{
    get
```

```
        {
            return txtLastName.Text.Trim();
        }
    }
```

Any command-line input and output is written as follows:

```
xcopy "MCMS_INSTALL_PATH\DevTools\NewProjectWizards80\Visual Web
Developer" "PATH_TO_MY_DOCUMENTS_FOLDER\Visual Studio 2005\Templates\
ProjectTemplates\Visual Web Developer"/E
```

New terms and **important words** are introduced in a bold-type font. Words that you see on the screen, in menus or dialog boxes for example, appear in our text like this: "clicking the **Next** button moves you to the next screen".

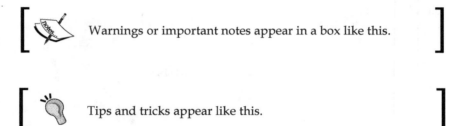

Warnings or important notes appear in a box like this.

Tips and tricks appear like this.

Reader Feedback

Feedback from our readers is always welcome. Let us know what you think about this book, what you liked or may have disliked. Reader feedback is important for us to develop titles that you really get the most out of.

To send us general feedback, simply drop an email to feedback@packtpub.com, making sure to mention the book title in the subject of your message.

If there is a book that you need and would like to see us publish, please send us a note in the **SUGGEST A TITLE** form on www.packtpub.com or email suggest@ packtpub.com.

If there is a topic that you have expertise in and you are interested in either writing or contributing to a book, see our author guide on www.packtpub.com/authors.

Customer Support

Now that you are the proud owner of a Packt book, we have a number of things to help you to get the most from your purchase.

Downloading the Example Code for the Book

Visit http://www.packtpub.com/support, and select this book from the list of titles to download any example code or extra resources for this book. The files available for download will then be displayed.

 The downloadable files contain instructions on how to use them.

Errata

Although we have taken every care to ensure the accuracy of our contents, mistakes do happen. If you find a mistake in one of our books—maybe a mistake in text or code—we would be grateful if you would report this to us. By doing this you can save other readers from frustration, and help to improve subsequent versions of this book. If you find any errata, report them by visiting http://www.packtpub.com/support, selecting your book, clicking on the **Submit Errata** link, and entering the details of your errata. Once your errata have been verified, your submission will be accepted and the errata added to the list of existing errata. The existing errata can be viewed by selecting your title from http://www.packtpub.com/support.

Questions

You can contact us at questions@packtpub.com if you are having a problem with some aspect of the book, and we will do our best to address it.

[5]

1
Installation

In this chapter we walk you through the installation and configuration of MCMS 2002 Service Pack 2 (SP2), along with SQL Server 2005 and Visual Studio 2005 on a single developer workstation. In addition, we will cover the changes to the SP2 development environment and a number of tips for working within it.

This chapter assumes you are already familiar with the steps necessary to install MCMS 2002 SP1a as detailed in depth in the previous book, *Building Websites with Microsoft Content Management Server* from Packt Publishing, January 2005 (ISBN 1-904811-16-7).

There are two approaches to setting up a development environment for SP2: upgrading from a previous SP1a installation, or starting from scratch and building a fresh installation including SP2. We will cover both approaches in this chapter.

For the examples in this book, we will be using Windows XP Professional SP2 as our development workstation. However, where there are significant differences for a Windows Server 2003 SP1 machine, those will be noted. All examples assume the logged-on user is a local machine administrator.

Overview of MCMS 2002 Service Pack 2

As with other Microsoft Service Packs, one major purpose of SP2 is to provide an integrated installation for a large number of previously released hotfixes. SP2 will now be a prerequisite for any future hotfix releases.

While many customers will view SP2 as a regular Service Pack, it also offers support for the latest development platform and tools from Microsoft, namely SQL Server 2005, .NET Framework 2.0 and ASP.NET 2.0, and Visual Studio 2005:

- **SQL Server 2005**: MCMS databases can be hosted by SQL Server 2005, offering numerous advantages in security, deployment, and most significantly, performance.

- **.NET Framework 2.0 and ASP.NET 2.0**: MCMS applications can be hosted within the .NET Framework 2.0 runtime, and take advantage of v2.0 language features as well as security and performance improvements. In addition, many of the new features of ASP.NET 2.0 such as master pages, themes, navigation, and Membership Providers can be used. This provides numerous opportunities to both refine and refactor MCMS applications, and is the primary focus of this book.

- **Visual Studio 2005**: MCMS applications can be developed using Visual Studio 2005. One of the greatest advantages here is the use of the new HTML-editing and designer features in VS.NET along with improved developer productivity.

If you wish, you can continue to use SQL Server 2000 for your MCMS applications. However, we recommend upgrading to SQL Server 2005 and will use it throughout the examples in this book.

There are numerous versions or Stock Keeping Units (SKUs) of Visual Studio 2005, all of which are supported with SP2. Throughout the examples in this book, we will be using Visual Studio 2005 Professional Edition.

Unfortunately, SP2 is not a cumulative service pack and therefore requires an existing installation of SP1a. Likewise, there is no slipstreamed distribution of SP2. The SP2 distribution is suitable for all editions of MCMS.

Mainly due to the extremely fast preparation and release of SP2 following the Release to Manufacturing (RTM) of .NET 2.0, Visual Studio 2005, and SQL Server 2005, the Microsoft installation information (KB906145) isn't particularly well documented and is somewhat confusing. Rest assured that the guidance in this chapter has been verified and tested for both installation scenarios covered.

Obtaining MCMS Service Pack 2

MCMS SP2 can be downloaded from the following locations:

- English:
  ```
  http://www.microsoft.com/downloads/details.aspx?FamilyId=
  3DE1E8F0-D660-4A2B-8B14-0FCE961E56FB&displaylang=en
  ```

- French:
  ```
  http://www.microsoft.com/downloads/details.aspx?FamilyId=
  3DE1E8F0-D660-4A2B-8B14-0FCE961E56FB&displaylang=fr
  ```

- German:
  http://www.microsoft.com/downloads/details.aspx?FamilyId=
  3DE1E8F0-D660-4A2B-8B14-0FCE961E56FB&displaylang=de

- Japanese:
  http://www.microsoft.com/downloads/details.aspx?FamilyId=
  3DE1E8F0-D660-4A2B-8B14-0FCE961E56FB&displaylang=ja

Installation Approach

We cover both an in-place upgrade to SP2 and a fresh installation in this chapter. Which approach you take is down to your specific requirements and your current, if any, MCMS installation.

If you wish to upgrade, continue with the next section, *Upgrading to Microsoft Content Management Server 2002 Service Pack 2* and then skip ahead to Chapter 2, *Getting Started with the Development Environment*.

If you wish to perform a fresh install, skip ahead to the *Fresh Installation of Microsoft Content Management Server 2002 Service Pack 2* section, about 18 to 20 pages into this chapter.

Upgrading to Microsoft Content Management Server 2002 Service Pack 2

This section details the steps required to upgrade an existing installation of MCMS SP1a, which includes the Developer Tools for Visual Studio.NET 2003 component. The outline process for an upgrade is as follows:

1. Install Visual Studio 2005.
2. Install MCMS 2002 Service Pack 2.
3. Configure the development environment.
4. (Optional) Prepare the MCMS database for SQL Server 2005.
5. (Optional) Upgrade SQL Server.
6. (Optional) Install SQL Server 2005 Service Pack 1.

We will perform all steps while logged on as a local machine administrator.

Installing Visual Studio 2005

Visual Studio 2005 can be installed side by side with Visual Studio.NET 2003. Once we have completed the upgrade, we can remove Visual Studio.NET 2003 if we wish to only develop MCMS applications using SP2 and ASP.NET 2.0.

1. Insert the Visual Studio 2005 DVD, and on the splash screen, click **Install Visual Studio 2005**.

2. On the **Welcome to the Microsoft Visual Studio 2005 installation wizard** page, click **Next**.

3. On the **Start Page**, select the **I accept the terms of the License Agreement** checkbox, enter your **Product Key** and **Name**, and click **Next**.

4. On the **Options Page**, select the **Custom** radio button, enter your desired **Product install path**, and click **Next**.

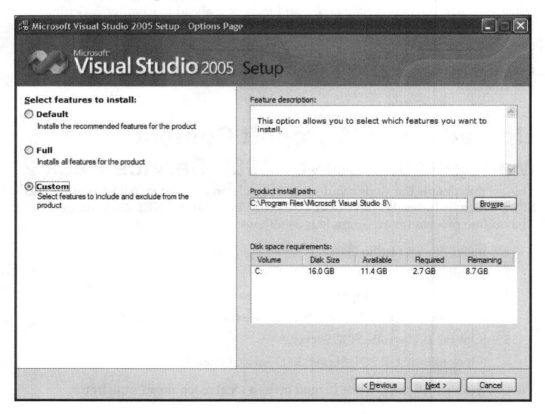

5. On the second **Options** page, select the **Visual C#** and **Visual Web Developer** checkboxes within the **Language Tools** section, and the **Tools** checkbox within the **.NET Framework SDK** section. Click **Install**.

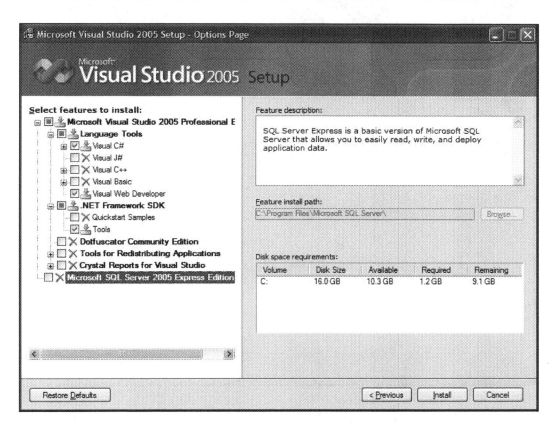

 Feel free to install any additional features you may wish to use. The above selections are all that's required to follow the examples in this book.

6. Wait (or take a coffee break) while Visual Studio 2005 is installed. When the **Finish Page** appears, click **Finish**.

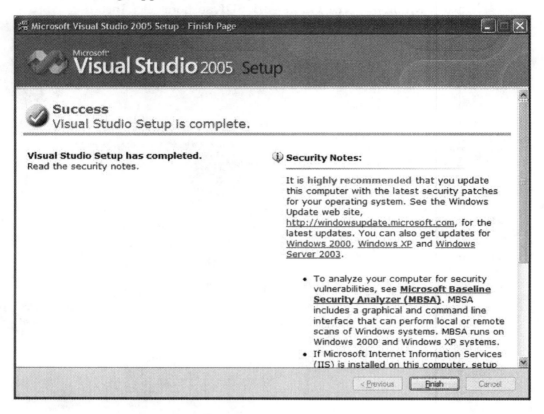

7. From the **Visual Studio 2005 Setup** dialog, you can choose to install the Product Documentation (MSDN Library) if desired.

8. From the **Visual Studio 2005 Setup** dialog, click **Check for Visual Studio Service Releases** to install any updates that may be available.

9. Click **Exit**.

Installing MCMS 2002 Service Pack 2

Next, we will install MCMS Service Pack 2.

1. From the **Start Menu**, click **Run...**

2. In the **Open** textbox, enter **IISRESET /STOP** and click **OK**. Wait while the IIS Services are stopped.

3. Double-click the SP2 installation package.

4. On the **Welcome to Microsoft Content Management Server 2002 SP2 Installation Wizard** page, click **Next**.

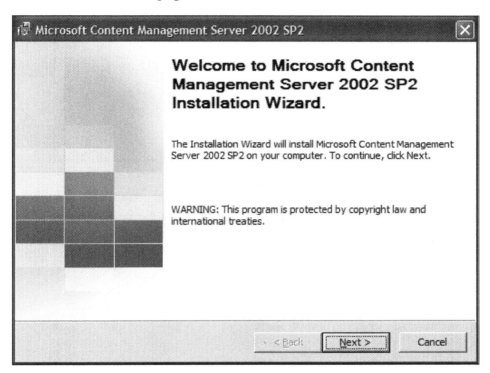

5. Select the **I accept the terms of this license agreement** radio button, and click **Next**.

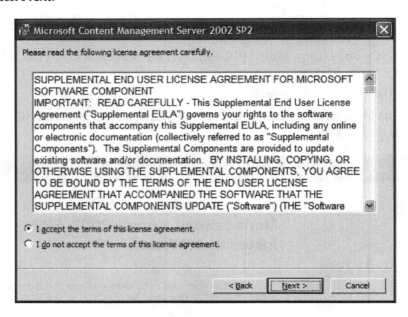

6. On the **ready to begin the installation** page, click **Next**.

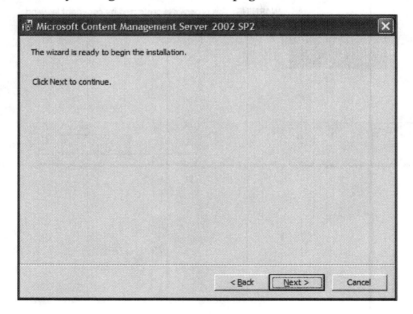

Wait while Service Pack 2 is installed.

7. During installation you may be prompted for the MCMS 2002 SP1a CD-ROM.

8. Once **The Installation Wizard has completed** page, click **Finish**.

9. If prompted, click **Yes** on the dialog to restart your computer, which will complete the installation.

10. Otherwise, from the **Start Menu**, click **Run...**

11. In the **Open** textbox, enter **IISRESET /START** and click **OK** to restart the IIS services.

 Stopping IIS prior to the installation of SP2 avoids potential problems with replacing locked files during the installation, and can prevent the requirement to reboot.

Configuring the Development Environment

Before continuing, a few additional steps are required to configure the development environment. We will:

- Configure the shortcut that opens **Site Manager** to bypass the **Connect To** dialog.
- Install the MCMS website and item templates in Visual Studio.

Site Manager Shortcut

During the installation of SP2 the **Site Manager** Start-menu shortcut will be overwritten. To configure **Site Manager** to bypass the **Connect To** dialog, take the following steps:

1. Select **Start | All Programs | Microsoft Content Management Server**.

2. Right-click the **Site Manager** shortcut and click **Properties**.

3. In the **Target** textbox, replace
   "C:\Program Files\Microsoft Content Management Server\Client\ NRClient.exe" http:///NR/System/ClientUI/login.asp
   with
   "C:\Program Files\Microsoft Content Management Server\Client\ NRClient.exe" http://localhost/NR/System/ClientUI/login.asp.

4. Click **OK**.

It is possible to configure many different **Site Manager** shortcuts pointing to different MCMS entry points. However, for this book we will only use the entry point on localhost, which is the only supported configuration for MCMS development.

Visual Studio Templates

The installation of MCMS Service Pack 2 automatically registers the MCMS developer tools such as MCMS Template Explorer in Visual Studio 2005. However, before we can create MCMS applications with Visual Studio, we need to make the website and item templates available.

1. Select **Start | All Programs | Microsoft Visual Studio 2005 | Visual Studio Tools | Visual Studio 2005 Command Prompt**.

2. Execute the following commands, replacing MCMS_INSTALL_PATH with the install location of MCMS (usually C:\Program Files\Microsoft Content Management Server) and PATH_TO_MY_DOCUMENTS_FOLDER with the location of your My Documents folder:

```
xcopy "MCMS_INSTALL_PATH\DevTools\NewProjectWizards80\Visual Web
Developer" "PATH_TO_MY_DOCUMENTS_FOLDER\Visual Studio 2005\
Templates\ProjectTemplates\Visual Web Developer"/E

xcopy "MCMS_INSTALL_PATH\DevTools\NewItemWizards80\Visual Web
Developer" "PATH_TO_MY_DOCUMENTS_FOLDER\Visual Studio 2005\
Templates\ItemTemplates\Visual Web Developer"/E
```

3. Execute the following command to register the templates with Visual Studio 2005:

```
devenv /setup
```

4. Close the command prompt.

This completes the steps to upgrade to SP2, and our environment is now ready for development! We can test our installation by viewing the version number in the SCA, connecting with **Site Manager**, or by using the Web Author. Of course, any existing MCMS web applications will at this time still be hosted by.NET Framework v1.1.

It is not necessary at this stage to register ASP.NET as detailed in the Microsoft Installation Instructions (KB 906145). This registration was performed by the Visual Studio 2005 installer.

Additionally it is unnecessary to configure IIS to use ASP.NET 2.0 using the Internet Information Services Snap-In, as Visual Studio 2005 automatically sets this option on each MCMS website application created.

However, if you are installing on Windows Server 2003, you must configure the Virtual Website root and the MCMS Virtual Directory to use ASP.NET 2.0, as it is not possible to use two versions of ASP.NET within the same Application Pool.

The ActiveX controls that are part of `HtmlPlaceholderControl` are updated with SP2. Therefore you will be prompted to install this control when first switching to edit mode.

If you have pre-installed the controls using `regsvr32` or Group Policy as detailed at `http://download. microsoft.com/download/4/2/5/4250f79a- c3a1-4003-9272-2404e92bb76a/MCMS+2002+- +(complete)+FAQ.htm#51C0CE4B-FC57-454C-BAAE- 12C09421B57B`, you might also be prompted, and you will need to update your distribution for the controls.

At this stage you can also choose to upgrade SQL Server or move forward to Chapter 2.

Preparing the MCMS Database for SQL Server 2005

Before upgrading our SQL Server installation to SQL Server 2005, we need to prepare the MCMS database so that it is compatible with SQL Server 2005.

1. Request the following MCMS hotfix from Microsoft: `http://support.microsoft.com/?kbid=913401`.

2. Run the hotfix executable to extract the files to a local folder, e.g. `c:\913401`.

3. Copy both of the files (`_dca.ini` and `_sp1aTosp2upgrade.sql`) to the MCMS SQL install folder (typically `c:\Program Files\Microsoft Content Management Server\Server\Setup Files\SQL Install`). Overwrite the existing files.

4. Delete the temporary folder.

5. Select **Start | Microsoft Content Management Server | Data Configuration Application**.

6. On the splash screen, click **Next**.

7. In the **Stop Service?** dialog, click **Yes**.

8. On the **Select MCMS Database** page, click **Next**.

9. In the **Upgrade Required** dialog, click **Yes**.

10. On the **Upgrade Database** page, click **Next**.

11. In the **Add an Administrator** dialog, click **No**.

12. On the **Database Configuration Application** page, uncheck the **Launch the SCA Now** checkbox and click **Finish**.

Upgrading SQL Server 2005

Before proceeding, be sure to have the details of your existing SQL Server Service Account, which you will need during the upgrade process.

1. Insert the SQL Server 2005 CD-ROM or DVD.

2. On the splash screen, click the **Server components, tools, Books Online, and samples** link within the **Install** section.

3. On the **End User License Agreement** dialog, select the **I accept the licensing terms and conditions** checkbox and click **Next**.

4. On the **Installing Prerequisites** dialog, click **Install** and wait while the prerequisites are installed.

5. Once complete, click **Next**, and wait while the **System Configuration Check** completes.

6. On the **Welcome to the Microsoft SQL Server Installation Wizard** page, click **Next**.

7. On the **System Configuration Check** page, all **Actions** should report a **Status** of **Success**.

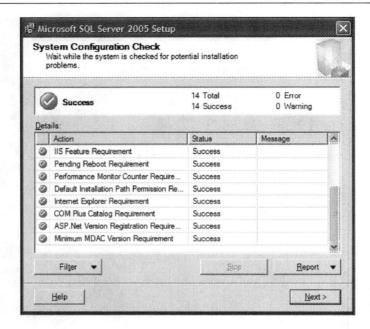

8. Click **Next** and wait while Setup prepares the installation.

9. On the **Registration Information** page, personalize your installation details, enter your product key, and click **Next**.

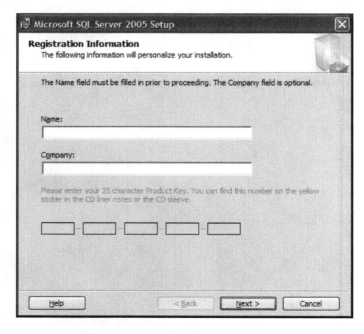

10. On the **Components to Install** page, select the **SQL Server Database Services** and **Workstation components, Books Online and development tools** checkboxes, and click **Next**.

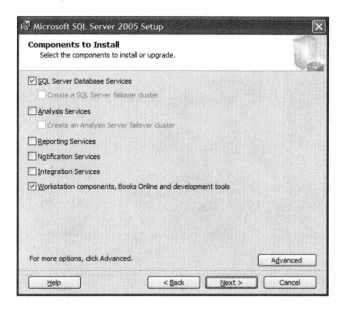

11. On the **Instance Name** page, select the **Default instance** radio button, and click **Next**.

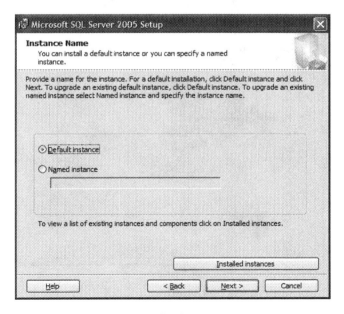

12. On the **Existing components** page, check the **SQL Server Database Services 8.00.2039** checkbox, and click **Next**.

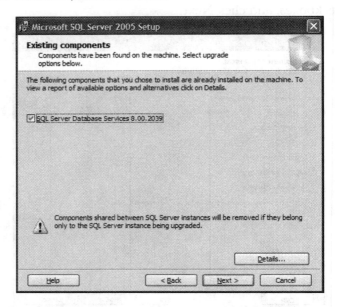

13. On the **Upgrade Logon Information** page, select the **Windows Authentication Mode** radio button, and click **Next**.

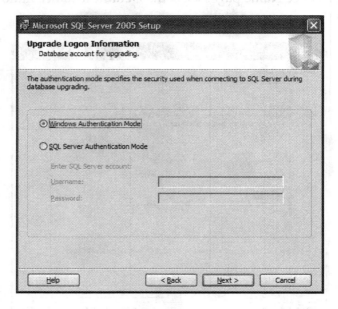

Wait while the upgrade is analyzed.

14. On the **Service Account** page, select **SQL Browser** from the **Service** combo box, enter your SQL Server Service Account details, and click **Next**.

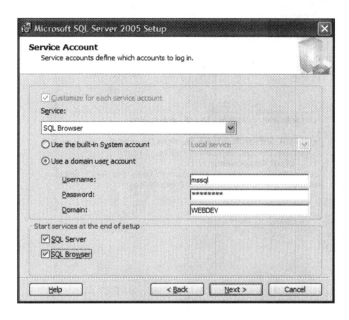

15. On the **Error and Usage Report Settings** page, choose if you would like to submit error and usage reports to Microsoft, and click **Next**.

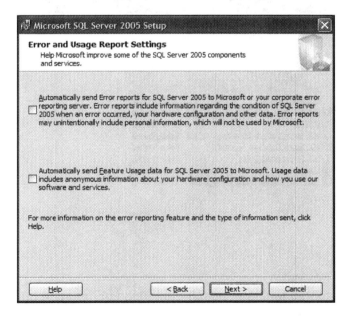

16. On the **Ready to Install** page, click **Install**.

17. Wait while SQL Server is upgraded, and click **Next**.

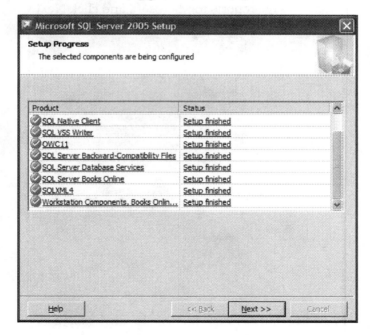

18. On the **Completing Microsoft SQL Server 2005 Setup** page, click **Finish**.

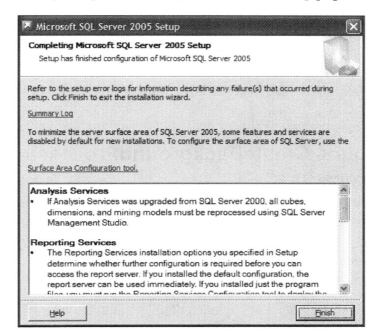

 To avoid possible ODBC errors while saving in the Web Author following an upgrade to SQL Server 2005, perform an **IISRESET** on the MCMS server machine. Note that for a production system, we would stop IIS before upgrading the SQL Server instance.

Installing SQL Server 2005 Service Pack 1

We will now install Service Pack 1 for SQL Server 2005, which can be downloaded from `http://www.microsoft.com/downloads/details.aspx?FamilyID=cb6c71ea-d649-47ff-9176-e7cac58fd4bc`.

1. Double-click the installer file, and wait while the files are extracted.
2. On the **Welcome** page, click **Next**.
3. On the **End User License Agreement** page, check the **I accept the licensing terms and conditions** checkbox, and click **Next**.
4. On the **Feature Selection** page, click **Next**.
5. On the **Authentication Mode** page, click **Next**.

6. On the **Ready to Install** page, click **Install**, and wait while the Service Pack is installed. During the installation, you may be prompted regarding **Pending Reboot Files**. If you are, click **Yes**.

7. When the **Locked Files Found** dialog appears, click **Continue**.

8. In the **Computer Reboot Required** dialog, click **OK**.

9. Click **Next**, and on the **Installation Complete** page. click **Finish**.

10. Restart your computer.

Modifying the CreateBackgroundProcessingJob Stored Procedure

Before proceeding, you need to modify one of the MCMS Stored Procedures to ensure its compatibility with SQL Server 2005.

1. Select **Start | All Programs | Microsoft SQL Server 2005 | SQL Server Management Studio**.

2. In the **Connect To** dialog, click **Connect**.

3. In the **Object Explorer**, expand the **Databases** folder, right-click the MCMS database, and click **New Query**.

4. Open Internet Explorer and navigate to `http://support.microsoft.com/default.aspx?id=906145#XSLTH3161121122120121120120`.

5. Copy and paste the SQL Script in the grey textbox to the **Query Window** in **SQL Server Management Studio**.

6. On the **SQL Editor** toolbar, click the **Execute** button.

7. Close **SQL Server Management Studio**.

This completes the steps to upgrade SQL Server 2005. You can now move ahead to Chapter 2.

Fresh Installation of Microsoft Content Management Server 2002 Service Pack 2

This section details the steps required to perform a fresh installation of SP2 using SQL Server 2005. All components are installed on a single machine and to their default locations. The following installation order provides all necessary prerequisites and is the optimal installation order from a time perspective. We start with a base installation of Windows XP Professional SP2, with all Windows updates installed. The outline process for the installation is as follows:

- Configure Local Security Policy.
- Create Service Accounts.
- Install Internet Information Services.
- Configure Internet Information Services.
- Install SQL Server 2005.
- Install SQL Server 2005 SP1.
- Configure SQL Server 2005.
- Bypass installation of Visual Studio.NET 2003.
- Install MCMS 2002 prerequisites.
- Install MCMS 2002 SP1a.
- Remove temporary items.
- Install Visual Studio 2005.
- Install MCMS 2002 SP2.
- Configure MCMS using the Database Configuration Application.
- Configure the development environment.

We will perform all steps while logged on as a local machine administrator.

Configuring Local Security Policy

In order to authenticate Service Account identities, we need to modify the Windows XP Local Security policy. Note that this section is not required if your machine is a member of a domain.

1. Select **Start | Control Panel**.
2. Double-click **Administrative Tools**, and double-click **Local Security Policy**. (If you do not see **Administrative Tools**, click the **Switch to Classic View** link.)
3. Expand the **Local Policies** node, and click the **Security Options** node.
4. In the **Policy** pane, scroll to locate the **Network access: Sharing and security model for local accounts** item and then double-click it.

5. Set the combo box to **Classic – local users authenticate as themselves** and click **OK**.

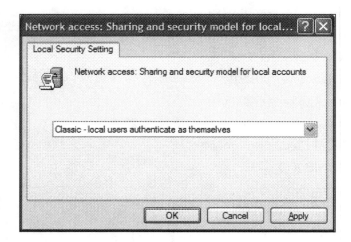

6. Close **Local Security Settings** and **Administrative Tools**.

Creating Service Accounts

We will create two Service Accounts, one for use by SQL Server and one for the MCMS System Account.

1. From the **Desktop**, right-click **My Computer** and select **Manage**.
2. In **Computer Management**, expand the **Local Users and Groups** node.
3. Right-click on the **Users** folder and click **New User…**
4. In the **New User** dialog, enter **mssql** in the **User name** textbox.
5. Provide a **Full Name** and **Description**.
6. Provide a **Password**.
7. Uncheck the **User must change password at next logon** checkbox.

8. Check the **User cannot change password** and **Password never expires** checkboxes and click **Create**.

9. In the **New User** dialog, enter **mcmssys** in the **User name** textbox.

10. Provide a **Full Name** and **Description**.

11. Provide a **Password**.

12. Uncheck the **User must change password at next logon** checkbox.

13. Check the **User cannot change password** and **Password never expires** checkboxes and click **Create**.

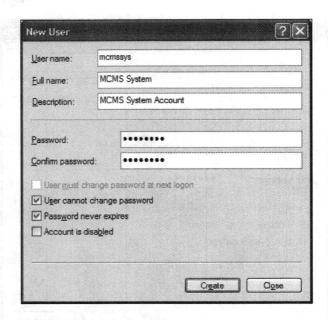

14. Close the **New User** dialog and close **Computer Management**.

Installing Internet Information Services

The following steps detail the installation of the minimal required components of Internet Information Services (IIS). Any differences to the procedure when installing on Windows Server 2003 SP1 are noted.

1. Select **Start | Control Panel**.

2. Double-click **Add or Remove Programs**.

3. Click **Add/Remove Windows Components**.

4. In the **Windows Components Wizard**, click (note: *not* check) **Internet Information Services (IIS)** followed by **Details…**

5. In the **Internet Information Services (IIS)** dialog, click (note: *not* check) **World Wide Web Service** followed by **Details…**

6. In the **World Wide Web Service** dialog, check the **World Wide Web Service** item and click **OK**.

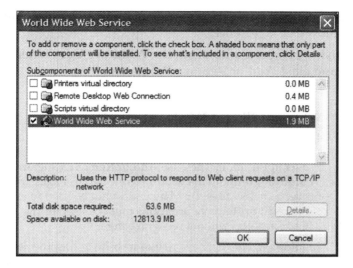

7. Ensure that the **Common Files, Internet Information Services Snap-In**, and **World Wide Web Service** have been selected. Click **OK**.

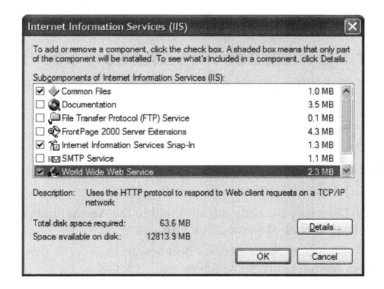

 It is not necessary to install FrontPage 2000 Server Extensions despite the requirement being stated in the product documentation, and during the installation of Visual Studio.NET 2003 later.

8. Click **Next** and wait while IIS is installed; you may be prompted to insert your Windows XP CD-ROM.

9. Click **Finish** when the **Completing the Windows Component Wizard** page appears, and close **Add or Remove Programs**.

When installing on Windows Server 2003 SP1.

Install the Application Server Role with ASP.NET (but not FrontPage Server Extensions) using the Manage My Server application. Then use **Add or Remove Programs**... **Windows Components** to add Active Server Pages and Server Side Includes. IIS Manager cannot be used to enable these; **Add or Remove programs** must be used or the MCMS installer will not recognize them!

In addition, create a new virtual website to host the Server Configuration Application. This site should be configured to use Windows Authentication and deny access from hosts other than localhost. Preferably this site hosting the SCA should also use Secure Sockets Layer (SSL). If this is not possible, configure the site to use a port other than 80.

Configuring Internet Information Services

We will initially configure IIS to use Windows Authentication. Later in the book we will explore alternative authentication methods.

1. From the **Start Menu**, click **Run...**

2. In the **Open** textbox, enter **inetmgr** and click **OK**.

3. Expand the **Local Computer** node, and the **Websites** folder.

4. Right-click **Default Website** and click **Properties**.

5. Click the **Directory Security** tab, and within the **Anonymous access and authentication control** frame, click **Edit...**

6. Uncheck the **Anonymous Access** checkbox and select the **Integrated Windows Authentication** checkbox, and click **OK**.

7. Click **OK**, and close **Internet Information Services**.

Installing SQL Server 2005

The following steps detail the installation of SQL Server 2005:

1. Insert the SQL Server 2005 CD-ROM or DVD.

2. On the splash screen, click the **Server components, tools, Books Online, and samples** link within the **Install** section.

3. In the **End User License Agreement** dialog, select the **I accept the licensing terms and conditions** checkbox and click **Next**.

4. In the **Installing Prerequisites** dialog, click **Install** and wait while the prerequisites are installed.

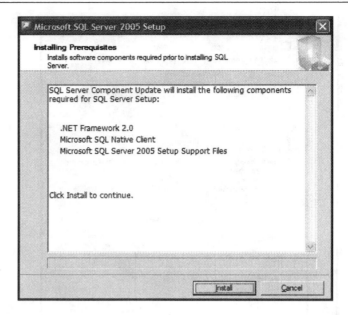

5. Once complete, click **Next**, and wait while the **System Configuration Check** completes.

6. On the **Welcome to the Microsoft SQL Server Installation Wizard** page, click **Next**.

7. On the **System Configuration Check** page, all **Actions** should report a **Status** of **Success**.

8. Click **Next** and wait while Setup prepares the installation.

9. On the **Registration Information** page, personalize your installation details, enter your **Product Key**, and click **Next**.

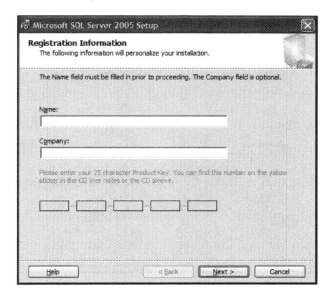

10. On the **Components to Install** page, select the **SQL Server Database Services** and **Workstation components, Books Online and development tools** checkboxes, and click **Next**.

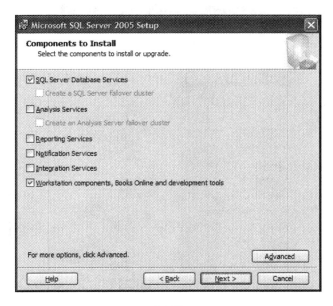

11. On the **Instance Name** page, select the **Default instance** radio button, and click **Next**.

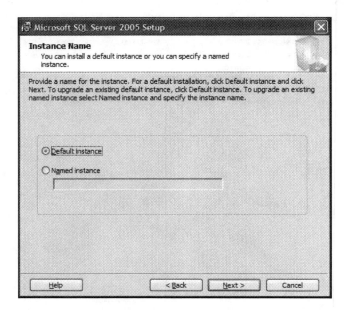

12. On the **Service Account** page, select the **Use a domain user account** radio button and enter the Service Account details for the **mssql** account. Check the **SQL Server Agent** and **SQL Browser** checkboxes, and click **Next**.

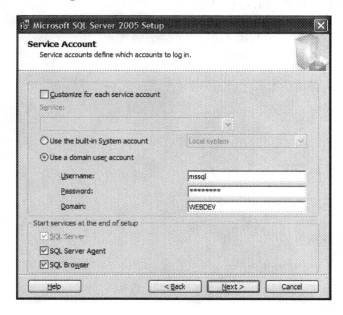

13. On the **Authentication Mode** page, select the **Windows Authentication Mode** radio button, and click **Next**.

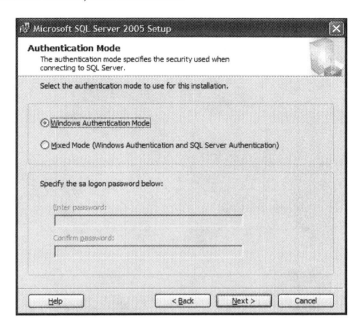

14. On the **Collation Settings** page, click **Next**.

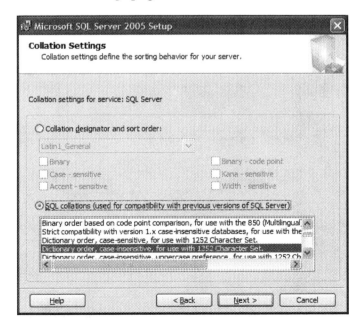

15. On the **Error and Usage Report Settings** page, choose if you would like to submit error and usage reports to Microsoft, and click **Next**.

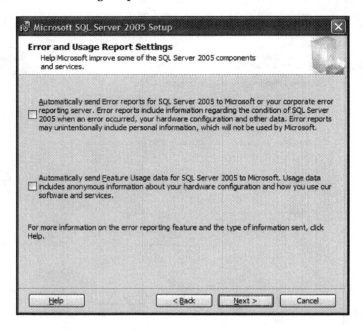

16. On the **Ready to Install** page, click **Install**.

17. Wait while SQL Server is installed, and click **Next**.

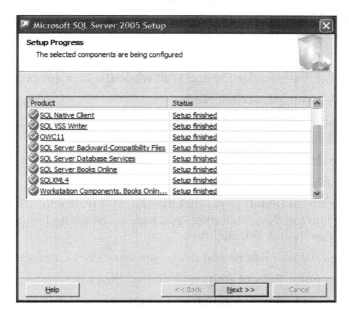

18. On the **Completing Microsoft SQL Server 2005 Setup** page, click **Finish**.

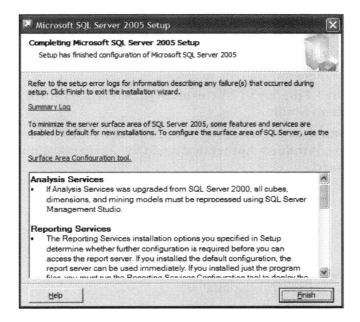

This completes the steps to install SQL Server 2005.

Installing SQL Server 2005 Service Pack 1

We will now install Service Pack 1 for SQL Server 2005, which can be downloaded from `http://www.microsoft.com/downloads/details.aspx?FamilyID=cb6c71ea-d649-47ff-9176-e7cac58fd4bc`.

1. Double-click the installer file and wait while the files are extracted.
2. On the **Welcome** page, click **Next**.
3. On the **End User License Agreement** page, check the **I accept the licensing terms and conditions** checkbox, and click **Next**.
4. On the **Feature Selection** page, click **Next**.
5. On the **Authentication Mode** page, click **Next**.
6. On the **Ready to Install** page, click **Install**, and wait while the Service Pack is installed. During the installation, you may be prompted regarding **Pending Reboot Files**. If you are, click **Yes**.
7. When the **Locked Files Found** dialog appears, click **Continue**.
8. In the **Computer Reboot Required** dialog, click **OK**.
9. Click **Next**, and on the **Installation Complete** page, click **Finish**.
10. Restart your computer.

Configuring SQL Server 2005

We will now configure our installation of SQL Server 2005 and create a database for use by our MCMS applications.

1. Select **Start | Programs | Microsoft SQL Server 2005 | Microsoft SQL Management Studio**.
2. In the **Connect to Server** dialog, select your server in the **Server name** combo box, **Windows Authentication** in the **Authentication** combo box, and click **Connect**.

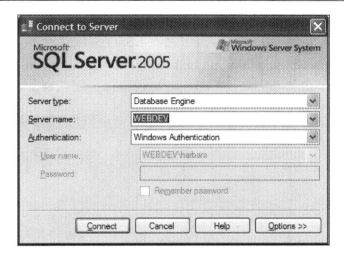

3. In the **Object Explorer**, right-click the **Database** folder, and click **New Database...**

4. In the **Database name** textbox, enter **TropicalGreen**, click **OK**, and wait while the database is created.

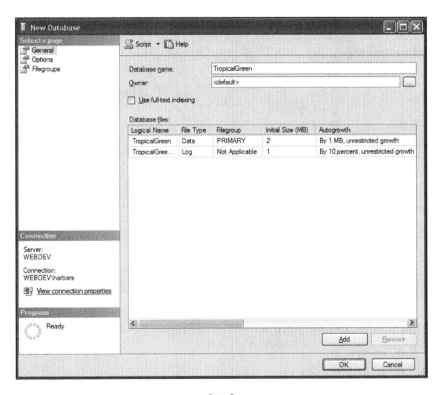

5. In the **Object Explorer**, expand the **Security** folder.

6. Right-click the **Logins** folder, and click **New Login...**

7. In the **Login name** textbox, enter **MACHINENAME\mcmssys**.

8. In the **Default database** combo box, select **TropicalGreen**.

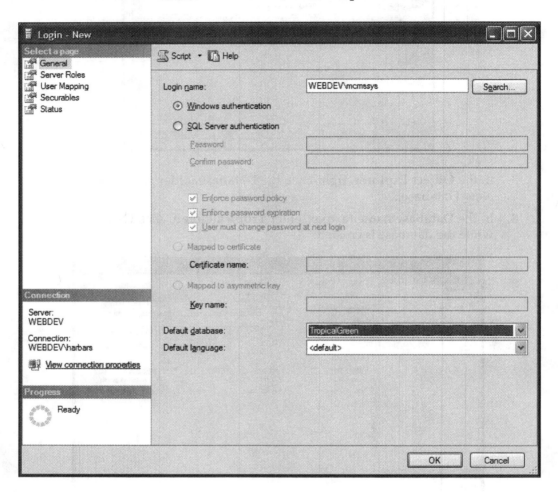

9. Click the **User Mapping** item within the **Select a page** pane.

10. In the **Users mapped to this login** grid, click the **Map** checkbox for the **TropicalGreen** database.

11. In the **Database role membership** grid, check the **db_datareader**, **db_datawriter**, and **db_ddladmin** checkboxes.

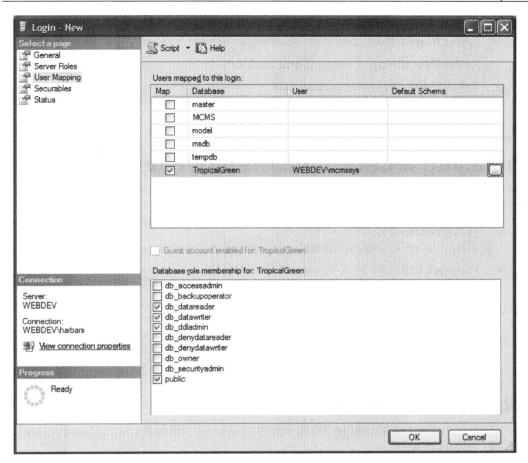

12. Click **OK**, and close **SQL Management Studio**.

Bypass the Installation of Visual Studio.NET 2003

MCMS SP1a requires an installation of a previous version of Visual Studio.NET to enable the Developer Tools component, prior to installing SP2. Installing Visual Studio.NET 2003 is both time consuming and undesirable. It is possible to bypass this requirement using the following procedure, which tricks the SP1a installer into thinking Visual Studio .NET 2003 is installed.

1. Request the following MCMS hotfix from Microsoft:
   `http://support.microsoft.com/?kbid=915190`

2. Run the hotfix executable to extract the files to a local folder,
   e.g. `c:\kb915190`.

3. Use Windows Explorer to create a folder, e.g. `c:\VSTemp`.

4. Select **Start | Run...**

5. In the **Run** dialog, type **cmd** and click **OK**.

6. Execute the following commands:

```
cd c:\kb915190
cscript VS2003ByPass.vbs c:\VSTemp
```

Installing MCMS 2002 Prerequisites

Before we can proceed with the installation of MCMS itself, we need to install two prerequisites. Installation of MCMS will be halted if these prerequisites are not met.

- **J# 2.0 redistributable**:
  Elements of MCMS Site Manager require the J# redistributable.

- **Internet Explorer Web Controls for MCMS**:
  Portions of the MCMS Web Author make use of the **Internet Explorer Web Controls (IEWC)**, of which a specific MCMS distribution exists for which compilation is unnecessary. These controls, unlike the standard IEWC, are supported as part of an MCMS installation. As they are a prerequisite for MCMS, IEWC can be utilized within your applications. However, ASP.NET 2.0 offers far richer controls for navigation, as we will see later in this book.

J# 2.0 Redistributable

We need to install the Visual J# 2.0 Redistributable to enable the installation of the MCMS **Site Manager**.

1. Download and save the J# 2.0 installer from: `http://www.microsoft.com/downloads/details.aspx?familyid=f72c74b3-ed0e-4af8-ae63-2f0e42501be1&displaylang=en`

2. Double-click the installer.

3. On the **Welcome to Microsoft Visual J# 2.0 Redistributable Package Setup** page, click **Next**.

4. On the **End User License Agreement** page, check the **I accept the terms of the License Agreement** checkbox and click **Install**.

5. Wait while J# 2.0 installs, and when the **Setup Complete** page appears, click **Finish**.

Internet Explorer Web Controls for MCMS

Internet Explorer Web Controls (IEWC) are required by the MCMS Web Author.

1. Download and save the IEWC installer from: `http://www.microsoft.com/downloads/details.aspx?FamilyID=FAC6350C-8AD6-4BCA-8860-8A6AE3F64448&displaylang=en`.

2. Double-click the installer.

3. On the **Welcome to the Microsoft Internet Explorer WebControls Setup Wizard** page, click **Next**.

4. On the **License Agreement** page, select the **I Agree** radio button and click **Next**.

5. On the **Confirm Installation** page, click **Next**.

6. Wait while the web controls are installed, and when **the Installation Complete** page appears, click **Close**.

Installing MCMS 2002 SP1a

1. Insert the MCMS 2002 SP1a CD-ROM, and on the splash screen, click **Install Components**.

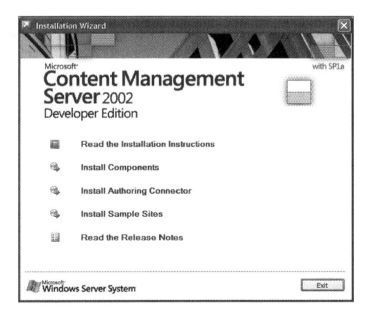

2. On the **Customer Information** page, enter your **User Name** and **Organization** along with your **Product Key** and click **Next**.

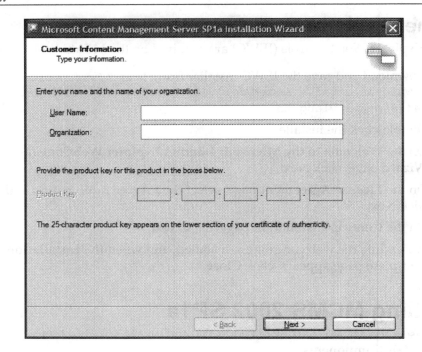

3. On the **License Agreement** page, click **Accept**.

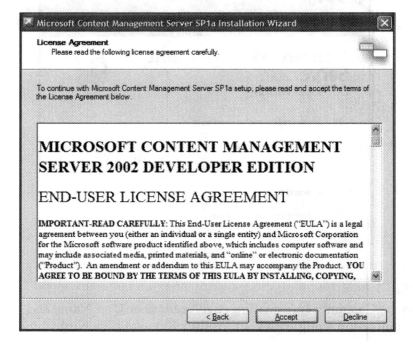

4. On the **Installation Options** page, select the **Custom** radio button and click **Next**.

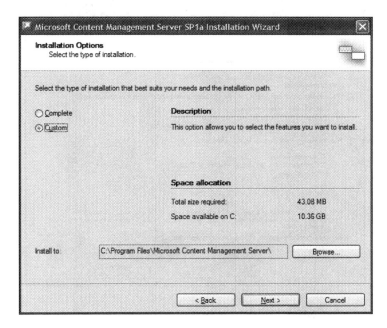

5. On the **Custom Installation** page, deselect the **Site Stager** item, and click **Next**.

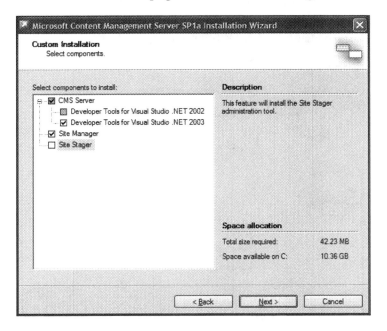

6. On the **Summary** page, click **Install**.

7. Wait while MCMS 2002 SP1a is installed.
8. On the **Installation Completed** page, uncheck the **Launch MCMS Database Configuration Application** checkbox, and click **Finish**.

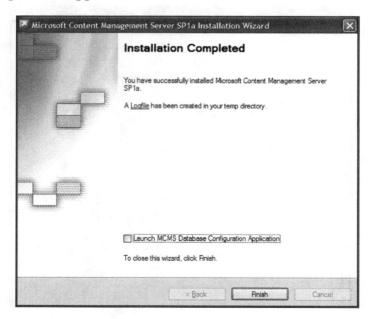

Remove Temporary Items

Now MCMS SP1a is installed, we can tidy up the temporary items we created earlier to trick the installer.

1. Select **Start | Run...**

2. In the **Run** dialog, type **cmd** and click **OK**.

3. Execute the following commands:

```
cd c:\kb915190
cscript VS2003ByPass.vbs c:\VSTemp remove
```

4. Use Windows Explorer to delete the folders c:\VSTemp and c:\kb915190.

Install Visual Studio 2005

1. Insert the Visual Studio 2005 DVD, and on the splash screen, click **Install Visual Studio 2005**.

2. On the **Welcome to the Microsoft Visual Studio 2005 installation wizard** page, click **Next**.

3. On the **Start Page**, select the **I accept the terms of the License Agreement** checkbox, enter your **Product Key** and **Name**, and click **Next**.

4. On the **Options Page**, select the **Custom** radio button, enter your desired **Product install path**, and click **Next**.

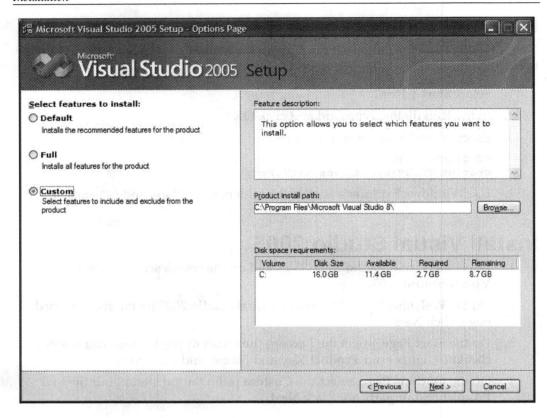

5. On the second **Options Page**, select the **Visual C#** and **Visual Web Developer** checkboxes within the **Language Tools** section, and the **Tools** checkbox within the **.NET Framework SDK** section. Ensure that all the other options are not selected and click **Install**.

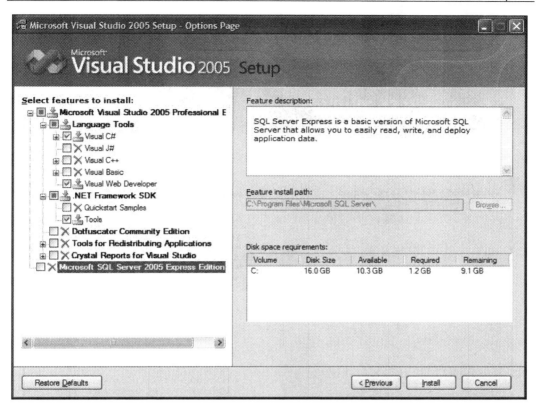

Feel free to install any additional features you may wish
to use. The above selections are all that are required for
following the examples in this book.

6. Wait (or take a coffee break) while Visual Studio 2005 is installed. When the **Finish Page** appears, click **Finish**.

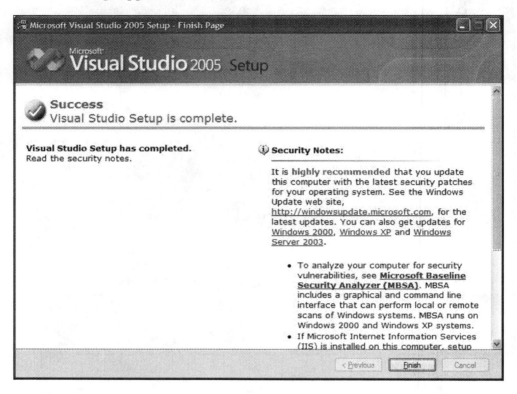

7. From the **Visual Studio 2005 Setup** dialog, you can install the product documentation (MSDN Library) if desired, otherwise click **Exit**.

8. From the **Visual Studio 2005 Setup** dialog, click **Check for Visual Studio Service Releases** to install any updates that may be available.

9. Click **Exit**.

Install MCMS SP2

1. From the **Start Menu**, click **Run...**

2. In the **Open** textbox, enter **IISRESET /STOP** and click **OK**.

3. Wait while the IIS Services are stopped.

4. Double-click the SP2 installation package.

5. On the **Welcome to Microsoft Content Management Server 2002 SP2 Installation Wizard** page, click **Next**.

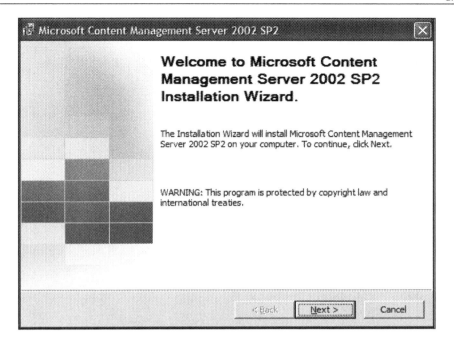

6. Select **I accept the terms of this license agreement** radio button, and
    click **Next**.

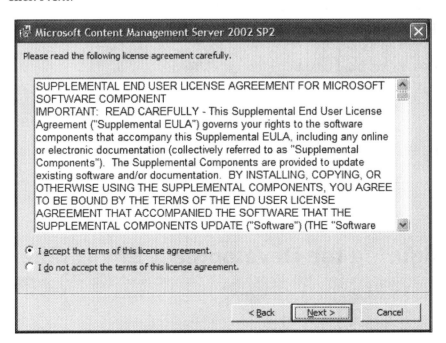

7. On **The wizard is ready to begin the installation** page, click **Next**.

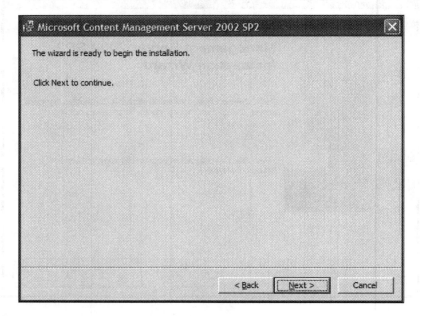

8. Wait while Service Pack 2 is installed.

9. On **The Installation Wizard has completed** page, click **Finish**.

10. If prompted, click **Yes** on the dialog to restart your computer, which will complete the installation.

11. Otherwise, from the **Start Menu**, click **Run...**

12. In the **Run** textbox, enter **IISRESET /START** and click **OK** to restart the IIS services.

Stopping IIS prior to the installation of SP2 avoids potential problems with replacing locked files during the installation, and can prevent the requirement to reboot.

Configuring the Development Environment

Before continuing, we need to look at a small number of additional steps required to configure the development environment.

Site Manager Shortcut

During the installation of SP2, the **Site Manager** Start-menu shortcut will be overwritten. To configure **Site Manager** to bypass the **Connect To** dialog, follow the steps here:

1. Select **Start | All Programs | Microsoft Content Management Server**.

2. Right-click the **Site Manager** shortcut and click **Properties**.

3. In the **Target** textbox, replace

   ```
   "C:\Program Files\Microsoft Content Management Server\Client\
   NRClient.exe" http:///NR/System/ClientUI/login.asp
   ```
   with
   ```
   "C:\Program Files\Microsoft Content Management Server\Client\
   NRClient.exe" http://localhost/NR/System/ClientUI/login.asp.
   ```

4. Click **OK**.

Visual Studio Templates

The installation of MCMS Service Pack 2 automatically registers the MCMS developer tools such as MCMS Template Explorer in Visual Studio 2005. However, before we can create MCMS applications with Visual Studio, we need to make the website and item templates available.

1. Select **Start | All Programs | Microsoft Visual Studio 2005 | Visual Studio Tools | Visual Studio 2005 Command Prompt**.

2. Execute the following commands, replacing MCMS_INSTALL_PATH with the installation location of MCMS (usually C:\Program Files\Microsoft Content Management Server) and PATH_TO_MY_DOCUMENTS_FOLDER with the location of your My Documents folder:

   ```
   xcopy "MCMS_INSTALL_PATH\DevTools\NewProjectWizards80\Visual Web
   Developer" "PATH_TO_MY_DOCUMENTS_FOLDER\Visual Studio 2005\
   Templates\ProjectTemplates\Visual Web Developer" /E

   xcopy "MCMS_INSTALL_PATH\DevTools\NewItemWizards80\Visual Web
   Developer" "PATH_TO_MY_DOCUMENTS_FOLDER\Visual Studio 2005\
   Templates\ItemTemplates\Visual Web Developer" /E
   ```

3. Execute the following command to register the templates with Visual Studio 2005:

   ```
   devenv /setup
   ```

4. Close the command prompt.

It is not necessary at this stage to register ASP.NET as detailed in the Microsoft Installation Instructions (KB 906145). This registration was performed by the Visual Studio 2005 installer.

Additionally, it is unnecessary to configure IIS to use ASP.NET 2.0 using the Internet Information Services snap-in, as Visual Studio 2005 automatically sets this option on each MCMS website application created.

However, if you are installing on Windows Server 2003 SP1, you must configure the Virtual Website root and the MCMS Virtual Directory to use ASP.NET 2.0, as it is not possible to use two versions of ASP.NET within the same Application Pool.

The ActiveX Toolbar control that supports the out-of-the-box Placeholder controls is updated with SP2. Therefore, you may be prompted to install this control when switching to edit mode for the first time.

You can pre-install the controls using `regsvr32` or Group Policy as detailed at `http://download.microsoft. com/download/4/2/5/4250f79a-c3a1-4003-9272- 2404e92bb76a/MCMS+2002+-+(complete)+FAQ. htm#51C0CE4B-FC57-454C-BAAE-12C09421B57B`.

Run the Database Configuration Application

At this stage, we are ready to configure MCMS.

1. Select **Start | Programs | Microsoft Content Management Server | Database Configuration Application**.

2. On the splash screen, click **Next**.

3. On the **Choose the MCMS Content Server ASP compatibility mode** page, select the **ASP.NET Mode** radio button and click **Next**.

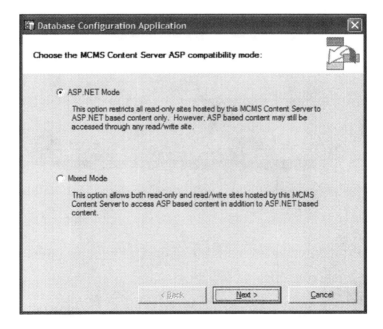

4. On the **Please select a virtual site for hosting the Microsoft Content Management Server** page, select the **Read/Write Site** radio button, and click **Next**.

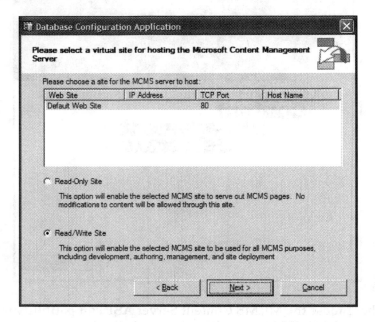

5. On the **SCA Web Entry Point** page, click **Next**.

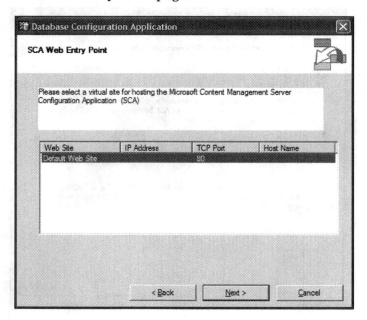

6. When prompted about a security warning, click **Yes** (as there are no means to further secure the SCA on Windows XP).

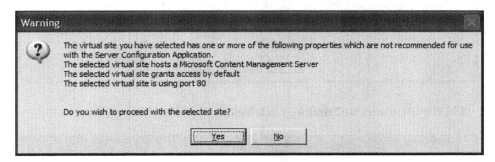

 When Installing on Windows Server 2003 SP1

Select the additional Virtual Website created earlier in the *Installing Internet Information Services* section as the SCA Web Entry Point.

7. On the **MCMS System Account** page, enter the account details as created in the *Creating Service Accounts* section earlier and click **Next**.

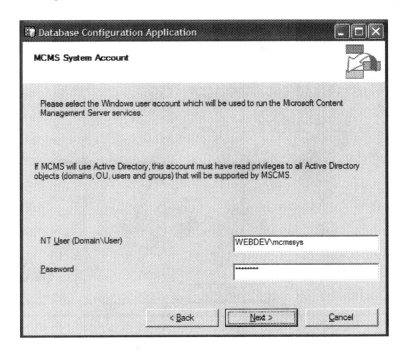

8. On the **Grant right?** dialog, click **Yes**.

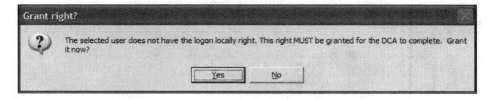

9. On the **Stop service?** dialog, click **Yes**.

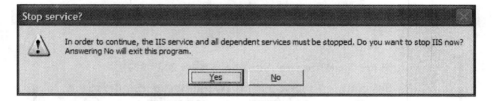

10. On the **Select MCMS Database** screen, click the **Select Database** button.

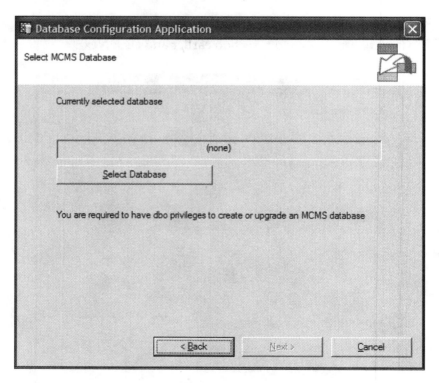

11. In the **SQL Server Logon** dialog, enter a period (.) in the **Server** textbox, and click **Options**. In the **Database** combo box, select **TropicalGreen** and click **OK**.

 A period (.) is the Netbios/RPC alias for the local machine. If the SQL Server Client libraries can determine that SQL Server is on the local machine, applications will use shared memory rather than a network protocol to access SQL Server when it is installed on the same machine as the application. This configuration can also be controlled using the SQL Client configuration utility.

12. On the **Select MCMS Database** page, click **Next**.

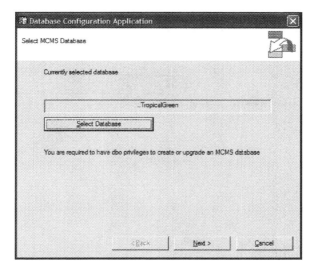

13. On the **Empty Database** dialog, click **Yes**.

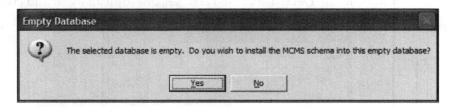

14. On the **Database Population** page, click **Next** and wait while the MCMS Schema is installed.

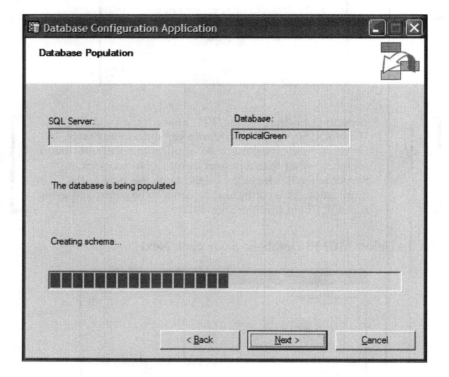

15. On the **Select Initial MCMS Administrator** page, enter the account details for the currently logged-on user, and click **Next**.

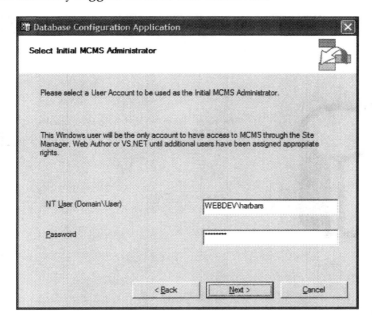

16. Wait while the changes are committed, and on the **MCMS Site Stager Access Configuration** page, click **Next**.

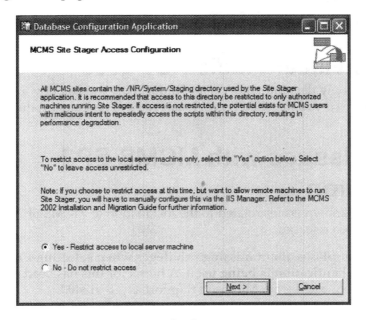

17. On the **DCA** dialog, click **Finish** to launch the **Server Configuration Application**, and verify your settings.

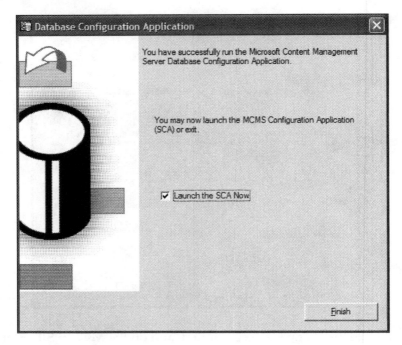

18. Close the **SCA**.

This completes the configuration of MCMS.

Remove Visual Studio.NET 2003

If you intend to only develop with Visual Studio 2005, you can now remove Visual Studio.NET 2003 (if you installed it previously) as it is no longer required.

Known Issues with MCMS SP2 Installation

There are a few known issues related to the installation of MCMS SP2 for which hotfixes have been released.

- **DCA complains about missing privileges when selecting a database when SQL authentication is being used**. A hotfix for this has been released and can be requested from Microsoft Support as KB 913400.

- **Developer tools for VS.NET 2003 disappear after installing MCMS 2002 Service Pack 2**. A hotfix for this has been released and can be requested from Microsoft Support as KB 914195.

- **Developer Tools for VS.NET 2003 do not work with some regional settings**. A hotfix for this has been released and can be requested from Microsoft Support as KB 914195.

In addition if you have performed a fresh installation of MCMS SP2 and wish to move an existing database to your new installation, you need to obtain the KB913401 hotfix and follow the steps detailed in the *Prepare the MCMS Database for SQL Server 2005* section under our discussion on upgrading to MCMS 2002 Service Pack 2 towards the beginning of this chapter.

Installation Tips

The following section provides two tips for installations on different editions of Windows or across separate machines.

Installing MCMS SP2 on Windows Server 2003 X64 Edition

MCMS Service Pack 2 introduces support for 64-bit versions of Windows Server 2003. However MCMS requires IIS to be configured to run in 32-bit compatibility mode. This means that all IIS applications (not just MCMS ones) cannot take advantage of the additional addressable memory on the X64 platform. In order to install MCMS SP2 on this platform, the following extra steps are necessary:

- ASP.NET 2.0 must be manually registered with IIS by executing the `aspnet_regiis` utility.

- IIS must be configured to run in the 32-bit compatibility mode, using the following command from the `c:\Inetpub\adminscripts` folder:

```
cscript adsutil.vbs set w3svc/AppPools/Enable32bitAppOnWin64 1
```

Installing the Required SQL Server 2005 Components

When making use of SQL Server on separate machine from the one running MCMS SP2, there is a prerequisite for SQLDMO, also known as SQL Server Client Tools, on the MCMS machine. This can be installed from your SQL Server 2005 distribution by:

- Clicking the **Advanced** button on the **Components to Install** dialog.
- Expanding the **Client Components** item.
- Selecting the **Legacy Components** item.

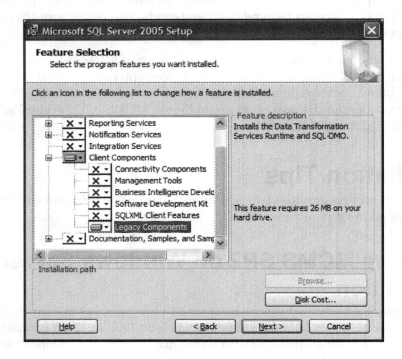

Summary

We have completed either an upgrade to SP2 or a new installation. In addition, we have covered the necessary configuration steps to avoid common problems with MCMS installation, seen how to avoid installing Visual Studio.NET 2003, and some additional installation tips. We are now ready to explore the MCMS SP2 development environment.

2
Getting Started with the Development Environment

Before proceeding, we will spend some time getting familiar with the MCMS Service Pack 2 development environment for Visual Studio 2005, which is slightly different from what we are used to with previous versions of Visual Studio. In addition we will create custom Visual Studio 2005 templates to overcome some of the issues that are present with the templates that shipped with MCMS SP2.

Visual Web Developer Websites

The key difference between developing MCMS applications with Visual Studio .NET 2003 and Visual Studio 2005 is that ASP.NET applications (and therefore MCMS applications) are now built using the Visual Web Developer component of Visual Studio 2005. Visual Web Developer introduces a new "project system", which no longer uses the project (*.csproj) files and simply accesses web applications via HTTP or the file system.

In Visual Studio .NET 2003, MCMS applications were created by choosing the **MCMS Web Application** project type. This project type was effectively a regular ASP.NET web application project with some modifications required by MCMS, such as additional references, the web authoring console, and modifications to the web. config. In Visual Studio 2005, developing web applications has been separated from developing other project types. The feature to develop a web application has been moved into the Visual Web Developer component.

To reflect this design change, you are no longer using **New Project** but **New Web Site** from the **File** menu in Visual Studio 2005 to create a new website.

Visual Studio 2005 ships with several website templates. The installation of the developer tools for MCMS extends the list of website templates with three additional templates: MCMS Empty Web Project, MCMS Web Application, and MCMS Web Service. These templates are actually modified versions of the similarly named standard templates shipped with Visual Studio 2005.

Creating an MCMS Web Application

Let's create an MCMS web application using Visual Studio 2005.

1. Open Visual Studio 2005.

2. From the **File** menu, choose **New**, followed by **Web Site…**

3. In the **New Web Site** dialog, select the **MCMS Web Application** within the **My Templates** section.

If the **MCMS Web Application** template does not appear in the **My Templates** section, the MCMS Visual Studio 2005 templates have not been correctly installed. Please refer to the *Visual Studio Templates* section of Chapter 1 for installation details.

4. In the **Location** combo box, select **HTTP**, and in the textbox, enter `http://localhost/mcmstest`.

MCMS applications have to be created using a local installation of IIS and do not support being created using the file system, which makes use of the built-in Visual Web Developer Web Server.

Note that the **New Web Site** wizard will not prevent you from configuring an invalid website using the File System and Visual Web Developer Web Server.

5. In the **Language** combo box (shown in the following figure), select **Visual C#**, and click **OK**.

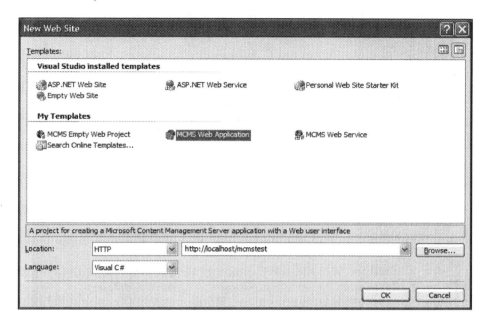

 If you wish, you can also choose VB.NET. The samples in this book are all written in Visual C#.

6. Visual Studio 2005 will create your project and initialize the MCMS Template Explorer. When it's done, you will be presented with an MCMS website with the basic foundation files.

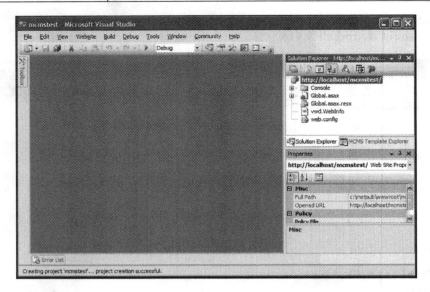

 The MCMS Template Explorer within Visual Studio 2005 logs on to the MCMS repository using the credentials of the currently logged-on user. If this operation fails, check your MCMS Rights Groups configuration. The Template Explorer does not allow you to specify alternative credentials.

7. Click the **MCMS Template Explorer** tab at the bottom of the **Solution Explorer**, and note that the **Template Gallery** is accessible.

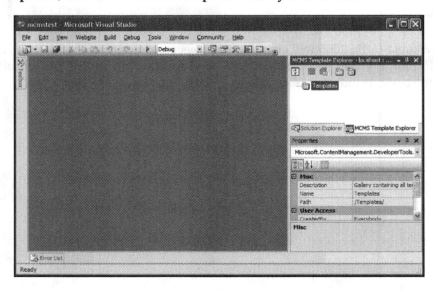

If you don't see the Template Explorer, it is likely you didn't select **HTTP** in the **Location** combo box in step 4. You may also not see the Template Explorer if you are using a locale other than US English, in which case you need to install hotfix 914195 as detailed in Chapter 1.

8. Click the **Solution Explorer** tab at the bottom of the **MCMS Template Explorer**, and click the **Refresh** button. Notice that unlike the web applications from ASP.NET 1.x days, the 'CMS' virtual directory is now part of the website.

9. If you examine the contents of the website, its references, and web.config file, you will see that the necessary MCMS files and configuration changes have been added.

Checking the Website Configuration Settings in IIS

We can verify that Visual Studio 2005 has configured the MCMS application correctly by using the Internet Information Services snap-in. First, let's ensure that the mcmstest website is indeed running on ASP.NET 2.0.

1. From the **Start Menu** click **Run**, enter **inetmgr** in the **Run** textbox, and click **OK**.

2. In **Internet Information Services**, expand the tree view to display the **mcmstest** application.

3. Right-click the **mcmstest** application and click **Properties**.

4. Click the **ASP.NET** tab and note that the ASP.NET version is correctly configured as **2.0.50727**.

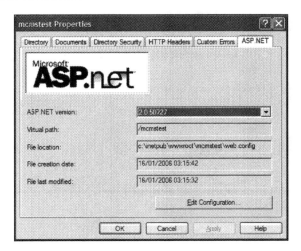

When developing on Windows Server 2003, the Virtual Website root must run in the same worker process (i.e. Application Pool) as all MCMS applications so that the MCMS ISAPI Filter can work as expected. This filter cannot route requests across worker-process boundaries. In effect this means that all MCMS applications will share the same ASP.NET version, as ASP.NET does not support side-by-side execution of different versions inside the same worker process. This is not necessary with IIS on Windows XP as it does not use Worker Process Isolation mode.

Next, we will check the authentication settings. For now, we will configure the website to use integrated Windows authentication. Only users with a domain or local user account will have access to the site. Later in Chapter 6 we will show alternative authentication methods such as Forms Authentication.

1. Click the **Directory Security** tab followed by the **Edit...** button, and note that the permissions are correctly inherited from the Virtual Web Site settings. In this example, we will use integrated Windows authentication.

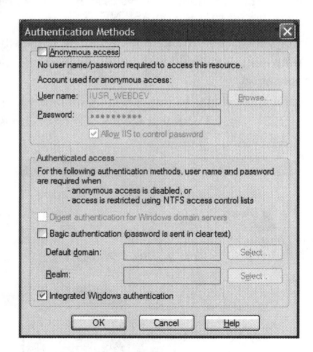

Note that we configured the Virtual Web Site to use Windows authentication in Chapter 1. Authentication methods can be configured on a per-application basis.

2. Click **Cancel** and close **Internet Information Services**.

Developing MCMS Web Applications

We are now ready to get started on developing our ASP.NET 2.0-based MCMS applications. There are a number of quirks with the MCMS web application templates, which we need to bear in mind during development.

1. Switch back to Visual Studio 2005.

2. In **Solution Explorer**, right-click on the website (**http://localhost/mcmstest**), and click **New Folder**.

3. Enter **Templates** as the folder name.

4. Right-click the **Templates** folder and click **Add New Item...**

5. In the **Add New Item** dialog, select the **MCMS Template File** item and enter **Basic.aspx** in the **Name** textbox. Click **Add**.

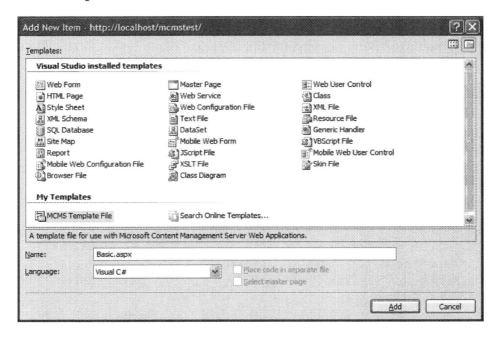

6. The new `Basic.aspx` template file is created and opened in **Source View**.

7. Examine the contents of `Basic.aspx`.

Correcting Basic.aspx

Notice that the `Basic.aspx` file has a few problems. Some elements are highlighted by IntelliSense "squiggles", and if we attempt to build the website, a number of errors will prevent a successful build. Let's correct the `Basic.aspx` template file.

1. In the `CodeFile` attribute of the `Page` directive on line one, replace `CodeFile="~/Basic.aspx.cs"` with `CodeFile="basic.aspx.cs"`

> The MCMS Web Application New Item template doesn't recognize that our new template file has been created in a subdirectory, and therefore the `CodeFile` attribute is incorrect. New templates in the web root are not affected.

2. From the **Build** menu, choose **Build Web Site**. Notice that the website now builds, but still includes a number of errors.

3. Correct the `DOCTYPE`. On line 19, replace
   `<!DOCTYPE html PUBLIC "-//W3C//DTD XHTML 1.0 Transitional//EN">` with
   `<!DOCTYPE html PUBLIC "-//W3C//DTD XHTML 1.0 Transitional//EN"`
   `"http://www.w3.org/TR/xhtml1/DTD/xhtml1-transitional.dtd">`.

4. Correct the `<html>` element. On line 20, replace
   `<html>` with `<html xmlns="http://www.w3.org/1999/xhtml">`.

5. Delete the comments on lines 4 through 17.

> The comments within an inline ASP script block (`<% %>`) are unnecessary.

6. Delete the `<meta>` tags on lines 10 through 13.
   ```
   <meta name="GENERATOR" content="Microsoft Visual Studio .NET 8.0">
   <meta name="CODE_LANGUAGE" content="C#">
   <meta name="vs_defaultClientScript" content="JavaScript">
   <meta name="vs_targetSchema"
   content="http://schemas.microsoft.com/intellisense/ie5">
   ```

These `<meta>` tags are unnecessary.

7. Correct the WebControls `Register` directive. On line 2, replace:

```
<%@ Register TagPrefix="cms" Namespace="Microsoft\
ContentManagement.WebControls" Assembly="Microsoft.
ContentManagement.WebControls"%>
```

with

```
<%@ Register Assembly="Microsoft.ContentManagement.WebControls,
Version=5.0.1200.0, Culture=neutral, PublicKeyToken=31bf385
6ad364e35" Namespace="Microsoft.ContentManagement.WebControls"
TagPrefix="cms"%>
```

 The original `Register` directive is not correctly recognized by Visual Studio 2005, and prevents IntelliSense from including the `cms` tag prefix.

8. From the **Build** menu, choose **Build Web Site**. Notice that the website now builds free of any errors and that the `cms` tag prefix is understood.

9. Your template file should now be as follows:

```
<%@ Page language="c#" AutoEventWireup="false" CodeFile="Basic.
aspx.cs" Inherits="Basic.Basic"%>

<%@ Register Assembly="Microsoft.ContentManagement.WebControls,
Version=5.0.1200.0, Culture=neutral, PublicKeyToken=
                                            31bf3856ad364e35"
Namespace="Microsoft.ContentManagement.WebControls"
TagPrefix="cms"%>

<!DOCTYPE html PUBLIC "-//W3C//DTD XHTML 1.0 Transitional//EN"
"http://www.w3.org/TR/xhtml1/DTD/xhtml1-transitional.dtd">
<html xmlns="http://www.w3.org/1999/xhtml">
```

```
<head>
    <title>Basic</title>
    <cms:RobotMetaTag runat="server"></cms:RobotMetaTag>

</head>

<body>
    <form id="Form1" method="post" runat="server">
    </form>
</body>
</html>
```

Configuring the 'CMS' Virtual Directory

You may have noticed during the previous example that it takes quite some time to build the website. This is primarily due to the fact that the contents of the 'CMS' Virtual Directory are included within the project. These files provide, among other things, the Web Author functionality, and are required by MCMS applications. However, their inclusion in the project causes some problems, as the files themselves do not need rebuilding. In addition, these files will generate a large number of warnings, and in some cases when additional elements are installed (such as the excellent Telerik r.a.d. MCMS Controls Suite), prevent a successful build. Let's configure the 'CMS' Virtual Directory so that it is ignored by the Visual Studio 2005 when building the website.

1. Open Windows Explorer.

2. Navigate to `C:\Program Files\Microsoft Content Management Server\ Server\IIS_CMS`.

3. Press *Ctrl+A* to select all four folders, and press *Alt+Enter*.

4. On the **Properties** dialog, click the **Hidden** checkbox.

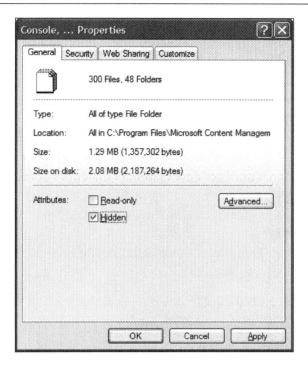

5. Click **OK**, and on the **Confirm Attribute Change** dialog, select the **Apply changes to the selected items only** radio button and click **OK**.

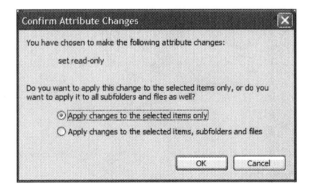

6. Close Windows Explorer.

Visual Studio will now ignore the content of the 'CMS' Virtual Directory when building websites, but the files will still be available to our MCMS applications. Remember to set the **Hidden** flag to all folders in the IIS_CMS directory if you install other third-party components into this folder in the future.

Creating Custom MCMS Application Templates

In order to save ourselves from the trouble of correcting the template file in the future, we shall create a new item template based on our corrected template. Start by checking if the **Export Template** item is contained within the **File** menu. If **Export Template** does not appear in the **File** menu, a common issue with Visual Studio 2005, take the following steps:

1. From the **Tools** menu, choose **Customize**. In the **Customize** dialog, click the **Commands** tab.

2. Select the **File Category** and scroll the **Commands** list box to locate **Export Template…**

3. Drag the **Export Template…** item onto the **File** menu.

4. Close the **Customize** dialog.

Now we can go ahead and create our custom template.

1. From the **File** menu choose **Export Template…**

2. On the **Choose Template Type** page, select the **Item template** radio button, and click **Next**.

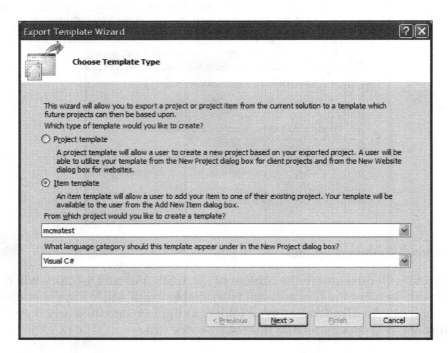

3. On the **Select Item To Export** page, select the **Basic.aspx** checkbox, and click **Next**.

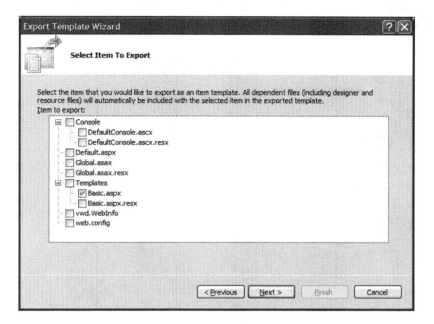

4. On the **Select Item References** page, click **Next**.

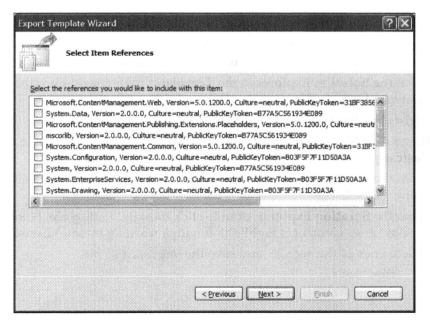

5. On the **Select Template Options** page, enter **MCMS SP2 Template File** in the **Template name** textbox, and a description (if you wish) in the **Template description** textbox. Deselect the **Display an explorer window on the output files folder** checkbox, and click **Finish**.

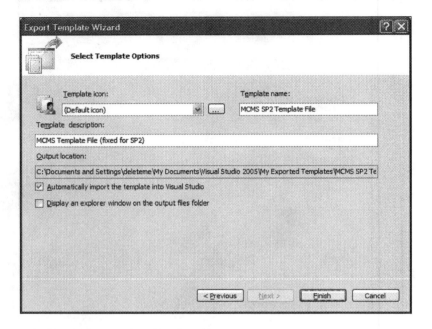

6. The new item template is created.
7. From the **Solution Explorer** in the **Templates** folder, right-click the `Basic.aspx` file and click **Delete**, followed by **OK**.
8. From **the Solution Explorer** in the **Templates** folder, right-click the `Basic.aspx.resx` file and click **Delete**, followed by **OK**.
9. Right-click the **Template** folder and click **Add New Item...**
10. In the **Add New Item** dialog, select the **MCMS SP2 Template File** item, enter **Basic.aspx** in the **Name** textbox, and click **Add**.
11. From the **Build** menu, choose **Build Web Site**. Note that the website build succeeds.
12. From the **Solution Explorer**, double-click the `web.config` file. Notice that the `<compilers>` element is highlighted with a warning by IntelliSense.
13. Delete lines 24 through 26, and save the `web.config` file.

```
<compilers>
. . .
</compilers>
```

The compiler element is not required and is no longer a valid entry within the compilers configuration section with ASP.NET 2.0.

Now that we have corrected all the problems with our MCMS SP2 application, let's build a Visual Studio 2005 project template.

1. From the **File** menu choose **Export Template...**

2. On the **Choose Template Type** page, select the **Project template** radio button, and click **Next**.

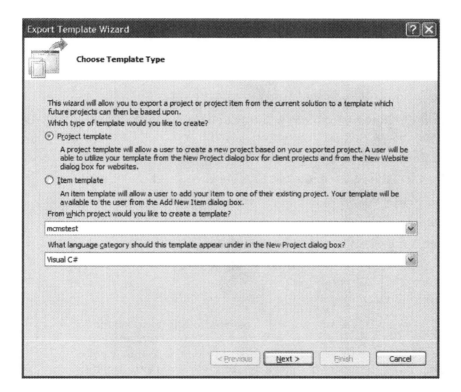

3. On the **Select Template Options** page, enter **MCMS SP2 Web Application** in the **Template name** textbox, and a description in the **Template description** textbox. Deselect the **Automatically import the template into Visual Studio** checkbox, and click **Finish**.

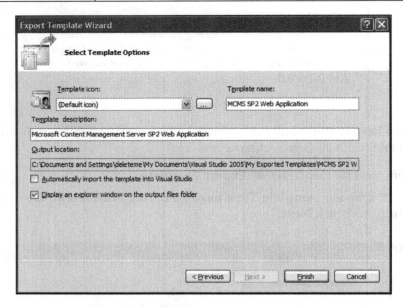

4. Switch to and close Visual Studio 2005.

5. In the Windows Explorer window opened by Visual Studio 2005, right-click the MCMS SP2 Web Application.zip file and click **Extract All...**

6. In the **Extraction Wizard**, click **Next**, followed by **Next**.

7. Deselect the **Show extracted files** checkbox and click **Finish**.

8. Delete the MCMS SP2 Web Application.zip file.

9. Double-click the MCMS SP2 Web Application folder.

10. Open the vwd.WebInfo file with Notepad.

11. Replace <UserProperties CmsEnabled="1"/> with <UserProperties CmsEnabled="2"/>.

> This setting allows Visual Studio 2005 to create the 'CMS' virtual directory when our application is created. It then sets the CmsEnabled attribute to 1. It may not be necessary to change this attribute if it is already set to CmsEnabled="2".

12. Save and close vwd.WebInfo.

13. Open the MyTemplate.vstemplate file in Notepad.

14. Delete line 17:

```
<Folder Name="CMS" TargetFolderName="CMS"/>
```

The export-template wizard automatically includes the contents of the 'CMS' virtual directory as part of the template; this step removes these files from the template.

15. Save and close `MyTemplate.vstemplate`.

16. Select all files in the `MCMS SP2 Web Application` folder.

17. Right-click the selection and click **Send To**, followed by **Compressed (zipped) Folder**.

18. Rename the ZIP file `MCMS SP2 Web Application.zip`.

19. Right-click the `MCMS SP2 Web Application.zip` file and click **Cut**.

20. Navigate to the `My Documents\Visual Studio 2005\Templates\ProjectTemplates` folder.

21. From the **Edit** menu choose **Paste**.

22. Delete the `My Documents\Visual Studio 2005\My Exported Templates\MCMS SP2 Web Application` folder.

23. Open a Visual Studio 2005 command prompt.

24. Execute the command `devenv /setup` and close the command prompt.

We have corrected the MCMS item and project templates which shipped with SP2, and are ready to create a simple test MCMS application based on our custom templates.

1. Open Visual Studio 2005.

2. From the **File** menu, choose **New**, followed by **Web Site…**

3. In the **New Web Site** dialog, select the **MCMS SP2 Web Application** item, select **HTTP** in the **Location** combo box, enter **http://localhost/mcmssp2** in the textbox, and click **OK**.

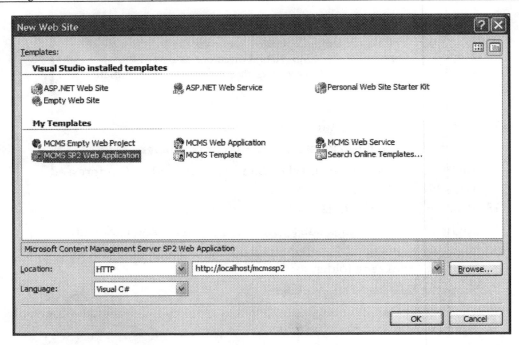

4. Open the **MCMS Template Explorer** using **View | Other Windows | MCMS Template Explorer**.

5. Right-click the **Templates** folder and click **New Template**.

6. Name the template **Basic**.

7. In the **Properties** window, click the ellipsis (**...**) button on the right of the **TemplateFile** property. If you do not see the **Properties** window, right-click the template and choose **Properties**.

8. In the **Select File** dialog, select the **Basic.aspx** file inside the **Templates** folder, and click **Select**.

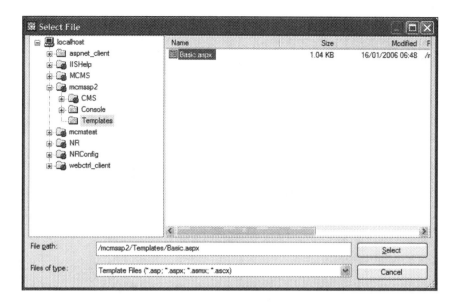

9. Click the ellipsis (**...**) button on the right of the **PlaceholderDefinitions** property.

10. In the **Placeholder Definition Collection Editor** dialog, click **Add**, followed by **OK**.

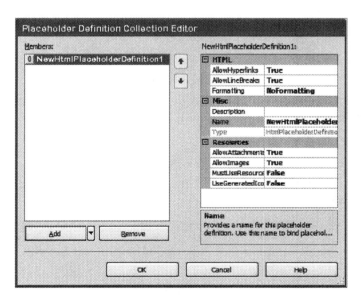

11. Click the **Save** icon at the top of the **Template Explorer** and click the **Solution Explorer** tab.

12. Double-click the **Basic.aspx** file inside the **Templates** folder and click the **Design** button at the bottom of the code editor.

13. Drag and drop **DefaultConsole.ascx** inside the **Console** folder from the **Solution Explorer** onto the design surface.

14. From the **Content Management Server** toolbox, drag and drop an **HtmlPlaceholderControl** onto the design surface.

15. Click the arrow on the **PlaceholderToBind** property within the **Properties** window, and select **NewHtmlPlaceholderDefinition1**.

16. From the **Build** menu, choose **Build Web Site**.

17. From the **Tools** menu, choose **Content Management Server** followed by **Web Author**. Internet Explorer will open at `http://localhost/channels`.

18. Click **Switch To Edit Site**.

19. Click **Create New Page**.

20. In the **Template Browser**, click **Templates** followed by the select icon for the **Basic** template. The new posting opens in Edit mode.

21. Enter some text into the HTML placeholder and click **Save New Page**.

22. In the **Save New Page** dialog, enter **test** as the **Name** and click **OK**.

23. Click **Approve** followed by **Switch To Live Site**. Note that the text entered in the placeholder is saved in a new posting.

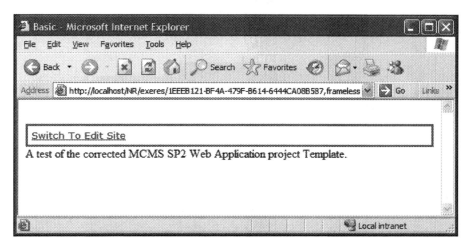

We have now tested our custom MCMS web application project templates. Before moving on, it is a good idea to tidy up our test files and projects. We can delete our test posting, its template gallery item, and the two MCMS applications we have created: **mcmstest** and **mcmssp2**.

Summary

We have reviewed the basics of the new Visual Studio 2005 MCMS development environment, configured the 'CMS' Virtual Directory, and have created our own custom Visual Studio 2005 templates for MCMS. We are now ready to dive into MCMS development with ASP.NET 2.0!

3
Using Master Pages

One the best features introduced with ASP.NET 2.0 is master pages, which allow developers to enforce common layout and behavior across pages within an application. While at first pass many master pages concepts are similar to those of MCMS templates, there are a number of benefits to be gained by taking advantage of master pages within MCMS applications.

This chapter provides an overview of the benefits of using master pages and a step-by-step guide for implementing them in your MCMS applications, where they become master templates!

Overview and Benefits of Master Pages

A **master page** includes common markup and one or more **content placeholders**. From this master page, new **content pages** can be created, which include **content controls** that are linked to the content placeholders in the master page. This provides an ideal way to separate common site branding, navigation, etc., from the actual content pages, and can significantly decrease duplication and markup errors.

Master pages make working with template files a lot easier than before. You can add common markup and shared controls such as headers, footers, and navigation bars to master pages. Once a master page has been built, you can create MCMS template files based upon it. The template files will immediately adopt the look and feel defined in the master template.

You can also mark certain regions of the master page to be customizable by introducing content placeholders (note that these are controls designed specifically for master pages and are not to be confused with MCMS placeholder controls). The space marked by content placeholders provides areas where you could add individual template markup as well as MCMS placeholder controls, as shown in the following diagram:

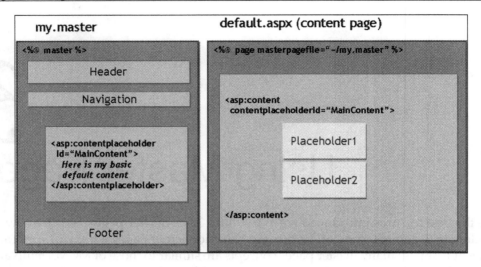

Although at first glance both master pages and MCMS templates offer a way to standardize the look and feel of a site, their similarities end there. Don't be mistaken into thinking that master pages take over the role of MCMS templates completely. A key difference between the two is that the use of master pages is reserved solely for site developers to ensure that template files created have a common look and feel. You can't create a master page and expect authors to use it to create postings.

In fact, master pages work alongside template files and offer a number of benefits to MCMS developers.

- **Avoids duplication in MCMS Template files**: Often MCMS templates contain common page layout code (usually an HTML table) along with navigation bars, headers, and footers (usually web user controls). This code has to be copied and pasted into each new template file after it is created or abstracted into user controls. In addition a change in the layout of this common code has to be applied to all template files. So, for example, an MCMS application with ten template files will duplicate this markup ten times. By placing this markup within a master page, this duplication can be removed.

- **Separation of site-wide markup from template markup**: One of the biggest drawbacks to MCMS is that the task of developing templates cannot be easily separated. It is a common requirement to separate the tasks of defining site branding, layout, and the development of controls such as navigation (performed by webmasters and programmers) from the task of designing template layouts (performed by business users). While master pages and Visual Studio 2005 do not address this completely due to MCMS's inherent architecture, they offer a substantial improvement in this area.

- **Avoids issues with MCMS Template File Visual Studio templates**: The MCMS Project Item Templates have a number of issues, and do not fully embrace the Visual Studio 2005 project system. Although any web form can be MCMS 'enabled', master pages offer a more seamless development experience with less manual tweaks required.

- **Visual Studio 2005 Designer support**: One of the common problems with using user controls within template files in Visual Studio .NET is that the template design view doesn't provide an adequate experience for template developers. Visual Studio 2005 offers an improved design-view experience including rendering of user control content, and this is especially valuable when working with master pages.

- **Experience of Master Pages**: Just as MCMS is a great way to learn ASP.NET, MCMS SP2 is a great way to learn ASP.NET 2.0! In addition, master pages are a fundamental building block of future Web Content Management offerings from Microsoft.

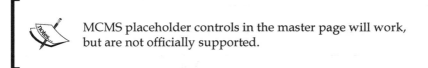

MCMS placeholder controls in the master page will work, but are not officially supported.

As we will see in this chapter, master pages provide an ideal way to separate common site branding, navigation, etc., from the actual content pages, and can significantly decrease duplication and markup errors.

The TropicalGreen Web Site

Tropical Green is the fictitious gardening society upon which the book's sample website is based. In the book, *Building Websites with Microsoft Content Management Server* from Packt Publishing (ISBN 1-904811-16-7), we built the Tropical Green website from scratch using ASP.NET 1.x.

In this book, we will attempt to rebuild parts of the website using MCMS SP2 and ASP.NET 2.0. While the code will be rewritten from the ground-up, we won't start with a blank database. Instead, we'll take a shortcut and import the TropicalGreen database objects from the `TropicalGreen.sdo` file available from the support section on Packt Publishing's website (`http://www.packtpub.com/support`).

Importing the TropicalGreen Site Deployment Object File

Before we begin, let's populate the database by importing objects using the Site Deployment Manager.

1. Download the `TropicalGreen.sdo` file from the book's companion website.

2. Open **Site Manager** and log in with an MCMS administrator account.

3. From the menu, select **File | Package | Import…**.

4. In the Site Deployment Import dialog, click the **Browse…** button. Navigate to the `TropicalGreen_Final.sdo` file downloaded earlier.

5. In the **Container Rules** tab, set the following:

Property	Value
When Adding Containers	Use package container rights
When Replacing Containers	Keep destination container rights

6. In the **Rights Group** tab, set the following:

Property	Value
Select how Rights Groups are imported	Import User Rights Groups

7. Click **Import**.

8. The import confirmation dialog appears. Click **Continue**.

Creating a New MCMS Web Application

To get started, let's create a new MCMS web application using the project templates we created in the previous chapter.

1. From Visual Studio, from the **File Menu**, choose **New | Web Site**.

2. In the **New Web Site** dialog, select the **MCMS SP2 Web Application** icon in the **My Templates** section.

3. Select **HTTP** in the **Location** list box.

4. Enter **http://localhost/TropicalGreen** in the **Location** textbox, and click **OK**.

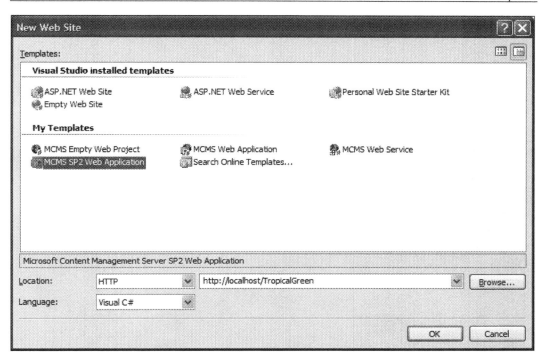

Our MCMS web application is created and opened in Visual Studio 2005.

Creating a Master Page for Use with MCMS

We will now add a master page to our MCMS web application and add the necessary elements for it to be usable with MCMS.

1. In the **Solution Explorer**, right-click your website and click **Add New Item...**

2. In the **Add New Item** dialog, select the **Master Page** template within the **Visual Studio Installed Templates** section.

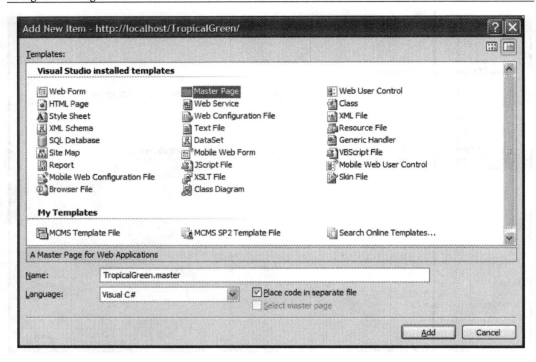

3. Enter **TropicalGreen.master** in the **Name** textbox, and click **Add**.

4. The master page is created and opened in the Visual Studio **Source View**.

In order to make use of MCMS controls such as the `RobotMetaTag` control within the master page, a `Register` directive is required.

5. Enter the following directly underneath the existing `Page` directive in the master page:

```
<%@ Register Assembly="Microsoft.ContentManagement.WebControls,
Version=5.0.1200.0, Culture=neutral, PublicKeyToken=31bf3856ad364e35"
Namespace="Microsoft.ContentManagement.WebControls" TagPrefix="cms" %>
```

Adding this `Register` directive in the master page allows us to use MCMS controls within the master page and prevents us from having to add it to the templates that make use of the master page.

Now MCMS controls can be added, and with full Visual Studio 2005 IntelliSense support!

6. Place the cursor directly below the `<title />` element within the `<head />` element.

7. Type **<cms:**, and IntelliSense will pop up. Select **cms:RobotMetaTag** and press *Space*.

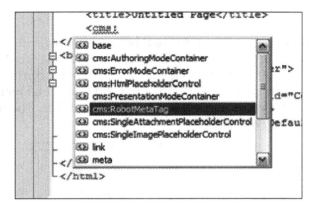

 The `RobotMetaTag` control is responsible for emitting the `robots` meta tags used by search engines to decide whether a page should be indexed, and whether the search engine should follow links on the current page. The values for these meta tags are controlled by the `IsRobotIndexable` and `IsRobotFollowable` properties of the posting. In addition, the control adds a `base` tag to the HTML content to ensure that relative references to files inside the template project can be found when a posting is requested.

8. Use IntelliSense to complete the tag by adding a `runat="server"` attribute.

The master page is now ready for any common layout, branding, and navigation elements. We will now re-create our TropicalGreen design, using a simple layout based on an HTML table.

1. Download the `Logo.gif` file from the book's companion website.

2. In **Solution Explorer**, right-click your website and click **New Folder** and name it `images`.

3. Add the `Logo.gif` file to the `images` folder.

4. We will configure the page to not have any margins on the top and left edges. Modify the `<body />` element as follows:

```
<body topmargin="0" leftmargin="0">
```

This markup will produce validation errors. We could avoid this by replacing it with definitions in a global CSS file. Themes and skins are covered in Chapter 5.

5. Enter the following code as you see it between the `<form>` tags, replacing the existing content. Include the text markers (e.g. `(Space for Console)`). The markers give us a visual cue to tell us where to place controls later. The page is formatted within a table, with the logo and horizontal menu at the top of the page and the vertical menu on the right-hand side. The rest of the space is for the main body or content.

```
<table width="100%" border="0" cellspacing="0" cellpadding="0"
height="100%">
<tr>
    <td width="100%" colspan="2" valign="top" bgcolor="#FFD300">
        <img src="/tropicalgreen/images/Logo.gif"/>
    </td>
    <td rowspan="10" valign="top">
        (Space for Console)
            </td>
</tr>
<tr bgcolor="#66CC33">
    <td colspan="2">(Space for Top Menu)</td>
</tr>
<tr>
    <td valign="top">
      (Space for SiteMapPath Control)<br/>
      (Space for Main Body)
    </td>
    <td class="RightMenuBar" width="20%" valign="top" height="100%"
                align="middle" rowspan="2" bgcolor="#669900">
      (Space for Right Menu Bar)
    </td>
</tr>
</table>
```

6. Toggle to **Design** view. Drag a **ContentPlaceholder** control from the **Standard** section of the toolbox and drop it in the table cell that contains the words **(Space for Main Body)**. Delete the text markers.

7. Save your work.

At this stage our simple master page contains the skeletal structure and layout of the page. It could be further modified to include any common elements required. For example, web controls can be used to add a common footer. Generally speaking, existing resources from MCMS applications can be reused without any issues once they are added to a website. However, careful consideration as to the best place to store such elements should be taken; for example, simply reusing user controls from a previous project may not be the best approach, as their content could be transferred to the master page.

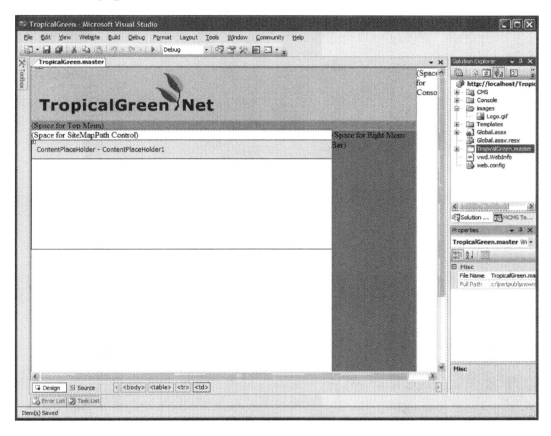

Now let's add the MCMS Web Author Console to our master page:

1. In **Solution Explorer**, expand the **Console** folder.

2. Drag and drop **DefaultConsole.ascx** onto the page directly after the **(Space For Console)** text marker, and then delete the text marker.

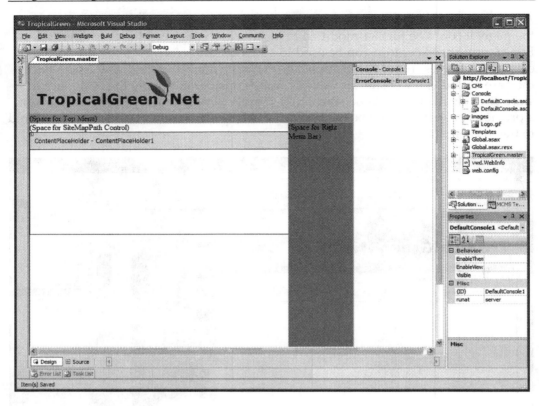

3. From the **Build** menu choose **Build Web Site**.

We have completed our TropicalGreen master page!

Creating an MCMS Template File Based on a Master Page

Now it is time to create an MCMS template file based on the master template that we have just created. We will create a plant template, which will be used within the TropicalGreen site to create fact-sheet postings about plants.

The fact sheet is a resource for hobbyists wishing to find out more about certain plants. Club members are avid gardeners. They often exchange gardening tips with fellow members. Younger green thumbs look up the information posted in the Plant fact sheet to tap into the wealth of experience that has been posted by fellow gardeners.

1. In **Solution Explorer**, right-click the **Templates** folder, and click the **Add New Item...** button.

2. Select **Web Form** template within the **Visual Studio Installed Templates** section.

3. In the **Name** textbox, enter **Plant.aspx**.

4. Select the **Select master page** checkbox and click the **Add** button.

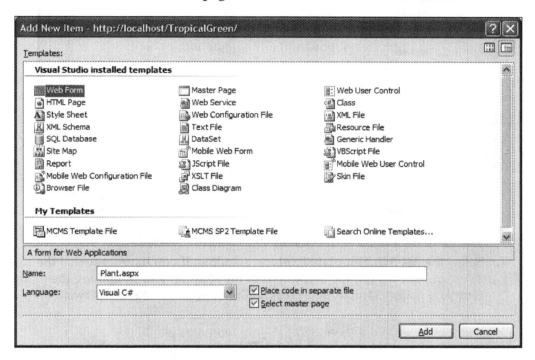

5. In the **Select a Master Page** dialog, select the **TropicalGreen.master** page previously created, and click **OK**.

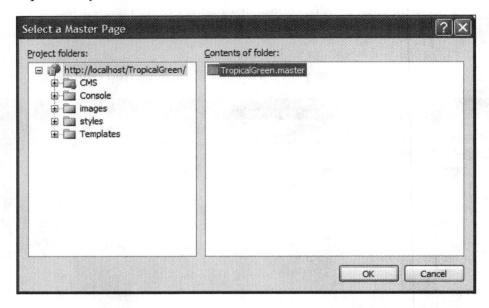

6. The template file is created and opens in **Source** view.

7. Select the **MCMS Template Explorer** window. If you have imported the TropicalGreen.sdo file at the start of the chapter, you should see the template gallery structure of TropicalGreen, which looks as follows:

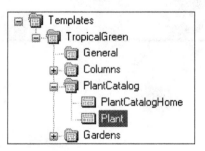

8. Navigate to the **TropicalGreen | PlantCatalog** template gallery. Right-click on the **Plant** template and select **Properties**. Ensure that the template is configured to have:

   o An **HtmlPlaceholderDefinition** named **Description** (click on the ellipsis in the **PlaceholderDefinitions** property field to show the **Placeholder Definition Collection Editor**).

- o A `TemplateFile` property value of
  `/tropicalgreen/templates/plant.aspx`.

9. Toggle to **Design** view. Drag a **Literal** control from the **Standard** section of the toolbox and drop it into the **Content** control. Set the **ID** of the control to **litHeader**.

10. Drag an **HtmlPlaceholderControl** from the **Content Management Server** section of the toolbox and drop it into the **Content** control below the **Literal** control.

11. Click **HtmlPlaceholderControl**, and set its **PlaceholderToBind** property to **Description**.

12. Save your work, and from the **Build** menu, choose **Build Web Site**.

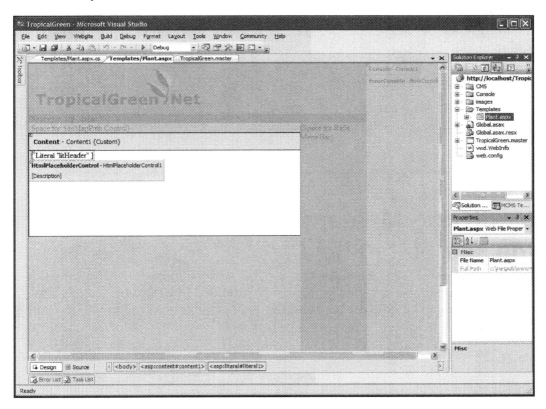

That's it! Our master-page-based MCMS template is now ready for use within the MCMS application by content contributors. At this stage any additional markup required could be added in the template file. The template can now be tested in the usual manner with the MCMS Web Author.

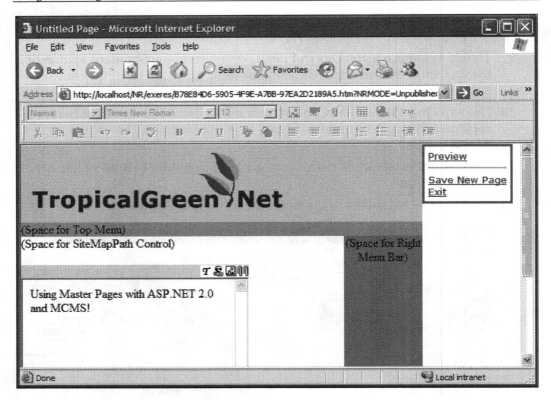

Modifying Master Page Properties from the Template File

You may have noted that the master page `<title />` element contained the text `Untitled Page`. Properties such as this can be modified from within the template file. Let's set the `<title />` element and the `litHeader` control to the MCMS Posting Display Name:

1. In **Solution Explorer**, right-click the `Plant.aspx` file, and click **View Code**.

   - Add the following `using` statement:

     ```
     using Microsoft.ContentManagement.Publishing;
     ```

   - Enter the following code within the `Page_Load()` method of the template file:

     ```
     string displayName = CmsHttpContext.Current.Posting.DisplayName;
     Master.Page.Title = displayName;
     litHeader.Text = displayName;
     ```

Code to manipulate master page properties can also be placed in the master page.

o   Save your work, and from the **Build** menu, choose **Build Web Site**.

We can now see that the Display Name is displayed in the Internet Explorer title bar as well as the ASP.NET Literal control.

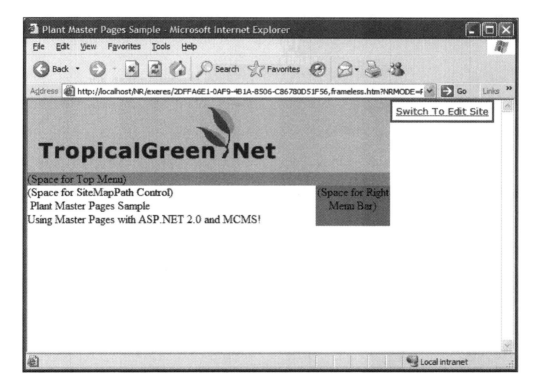

Summary

We have covered the basics of ASP.NET 2.0 master pages, created our first MCMS master template, and seen the numerous benefits these offer to MCMS developers, including greatly enhanced design-time experience and removal of markup duplication. By using master pages, you can enforce design consistency, reduce code, and enjoy a rich design-time experience while developing MCMS applications.

4
Navigation Controls

Developing site navigation is an exercise that often leaves developers in a dilemma. Early versions of Visual Studio did not provide any ready-to-use navigation controls. Developers had to choose between spending many hours building controls from scratch or expanding project budgets to purchase shrink-wrapped software. While free controls were available for download from the Internet, they weren't always ready for use, and developers still had to spend a fair bit of time understanding the code and customizing it to fit their requirements.

The good news is: ASP.NET 2.0 introduces a whole new way of implementing site navigation. Packaged as part of ASP.NET 2.0 are three powerful navigation controls:

- The `SiteMapPath` control generates a series of links that connect to one another on a website, for example, **Home > Plant Catalog > Aloe Vera**.

  It is the "You Are Here" sign that tells visitors exactly where they are. It is also sometimes known as a breadcrumb trail, and like the trail of breadcrumbs left by the fictional characters Hansel and Gretel, it helps users find their way back from the main page.

- The `Menu` control can be configured to show static horizontal or vertical lists of items. It can even be dynamic, showing and hiding sub-items when the cursor hovers over an item.

- The `TreeView` control provides a hierarchical representation of the site. It contains a list of all items on the site nested in a tree. Users can click to expand leaf nodes to reveal sub-nodes.

All of the above listed controls can be driven by site maps. You can think of site maps as a collection of items that make up the structure of your site. By programmatically adding channels and postings to a site map, we are able to smoothly integrate these controls to any MCMS site as we will see in this chapter.

Navigation for TropicalGreen

In the book, *Building Websites with Microsoft Content Management Server*
from Packt Publishing (ISBN 1-904811-16-7), we designed TropicalGreen to display:

- A horizontal menu with the following items:
  - Home
  - Help
  - Site map
- A vertical menu with the following items:
  - Columns
  - Gardens
  - Plant catalog
- A SiteMapPath control (or breadcrumb trail)
- A TreeView control for the site map
- A listing for summary pages

Let's attempt to re-create this navigation structure using the controls available in
ASP.NET 2.0. At the end of the chapter, the TropicalGreen site will contain each
element as shown in the following screenshot:

Site Maps and Site-Map Providers

Site maps contain a collection of items to be included as part of the website's navigation structure. The items are usually displayed in a hierarchical tree-like structure. In MCMS, this would usually be a list of channels and postings or sometimes galleries, resources, and templates. In its simplest form, a site map can be a plain XML file that stores a list of nodes, such as the following:

```
<?xml version="1.0" encoding="utf-8"?>
<siteMap xmlns="http://schemas.microsoft.com/AspNet/SiteMap-File-1.0">
  <siteMapNode url="http://tropicalgreen/" title="Home"/>
    <siteMapNode url="/PlantCatalog/" title="Plant Catalog">
    <siteMapNode url="/Gardens/" title="Gardens">
      <siteMapNode url="/Gardens/Members/" title="Members"/>
    </siteMapNode>

    . . . code continues . . .

  </siteMapNode>
</siteMap>
```

After defining the site map, you could add a SiteMapDataSource to the page together with, say, a Menu control, bind the site map data source to the Menu control, and the contents of the XML file will get translated into menu items. Of course, the conversion of XML nodes to menu items is not magical. Behind the scenes, a SiteMapProvider (specifically, the XmlSiteMapProvider) reads the XML file and programmatically loads each node into the SiteMapDataSource.

While we could use an XML file to hold the list of nodes, it would merely be a static snapshot of the site's structure. When new channels or pages are added or deleted, the file has to be updated accordingly. Hardcoding nodes and links in an XML file may work well on sites with a relatively fixed structure. However, for many MCMS websites where channels and pages are added and deleted frequently or where different users might be allowed to see a different set of pages, a more dynamic approach would be preferred.

As the XmlSiteMapProvider is the only provider that ships with ASP.NET 2.0, we will need to build a custom site-map provider to read from the MCMS repository.

The custom site-map provider will use the MCMS **Publishing Application Programming Interface (PAPI)** to retrieve the channels and postings from the MCMS repository to form the site map. The benefit of this approach is that security trimming is automatically provided by PAPI, as only the items that the current user is allowed to see will be retrieved.

Building an MCMS Site-Map Provider

To build a custom `SiteMapProvider`, we will create a class that inherits from the base `SiteMapProvider` class and implement four methods inherited from the base:

- The `FindSiteMapNode()` method returns a site map node based on a given URL or GUID.
- The `GetChildNodes()` method returns a collection of nodes of a specified parent node.
- The `GetParentNode()` method returns the parent node of a specified child.
- The `GetRootNodeCore()` method returns the first node in the hierarchy.

As the navigation controls for the TropicalGreen site provide links to channel items, each site map node maps to a corresponding channel item. Nevertheless, you can easily modify the methods to display template gallery items or resource gallery items instead. Now, let's proceed to build the `MCMSSiteMapProvider` class.

The MCMSSiteMapProvider Class

To keep things simple, we can take advantage of another new capability within ASP. NET: the `App_Code` folder. The `App_Code` folder also allows us to add functionality without the need to rebuild our website.

1. First, if you have not already done so, add the `App_Code` ASP.NET folder to the TropicalGreen solution. Right-click on the project and select **Add | ASP. NET folder | App_Code**.

2. Within the `App_Code` folder create a new sub-folder named `SiteMapProviders`.

3. Right-click the newly created `SiteMapProviders` folder and add a class file named `MCMSSiteMapProvider.cs`.

4. The code requires the use of methods from the highlighted namespace (in the code snippet that follows); so add it to the class file. Add also the namespace declaration.

```
using System;
using System.Data;
using System.Configuration;
using System.Web;
using System.Web.Security;
```

```
using System.Web.UI;
using System.Web.UI.WebControls;
using System.Web.UI.WebControls.WebParts;
using System.Web.UI.HtmlControls;
using Microsoft.ContentManagement.Publishing;

namespace TropicalGreen
{
        public class MCMSSiteMapProvider
    {
        . . . code continues . . .
    }
}
```

5. Since there aren't any ready-to-use `SiteMapProvider`s that works with MCMS objects, the custom provider will inherit from the base `SiteMapProvider` class.

```
public class MCMSSiteMapProvider : SiteMapProvider
{
    . . . code continues . . .
}
```

6. We will also add a private variable named `rootPath` to store the path of the top-level channel. For TropicalGreen, the path is `/Channels/tropicalgreen/`. Add the highlighted code within the class declaration.

```
public class MCMSSiteMapProvider : SiteMapProvider
{
    protected string RootChannel = "/Channels/tropicalgreen/";

    . . . code continues . . .
}
```

Alternatively, we could store the path to the channel in the `<appSettings>` section of the `web.config` file. That will make it easier for the code to be reused in other solutions, as we won't have to recompile the code each time the path changes.

7. Finally, remove the class constructor (code as follows). It is not required.

```
public MCMSSiteMapProvider()
{
    //
    // TODO: Add constructor logic here
    //
}
```

Implementing the GetRootNodeCore() Method

The GetRootNodeCore() method returns the first node in the hierarchy. In the case of the TropicalGreen site, the first node is that of the first-level channel, TropicalGreen. We've already stored its path in the class variable rootChannel. We use the Searches.GetByPath() method from the PAPI to return an instance of the TropicalGreen channel. Add the GetRootNodeCore() method to the class.

```
protected override SiteMapNode GetRootNodeCore()
{
    Channel root = CmsHttpContext.Current.Searches.GetByPath
                   (RootChannel) as Channel;
    return GetSiteMapNodeFromChannelItem(root);
}
```

Notice that in the code, we used a method named GetSiteMapNodeFromChannelItem() to create a site map node based on a channel item. A site map node has four essential properties:

- Key: A value to uniquely identify the node. We will set it to the channel item's GUID.
- Url: Specifies the address of the node, which for our site will be the URL of the channel item.
- Title: Specifies the text label that will be used to display the node. We retrieve the channel item's display name and use it for the title.
- Description: Specifies the contents of the tool tip that will be shown when the mouse is placed over the node. Especially useful for providing visitors a description about the page behind the link.

From the channel item, we will create a site map node based on the properties discussed in the previous list. Append the GetSiteMapNodeFromChannelItem() method to the class file.

```
protected SiteMapNode GetSiteMapNodeFromChannelItem(ChannelItem ci)
{
    SiteMapNode smn = null;
    if (ci != null)
    {
        smn = new SiteMapNode(this, ci.Guid);
        smn.Url = ci.Url;
        smn.Title = ci.DisplayName;
        smn.Description = ci.Description;
    }
```

```
    return smn;
}
```

Implementing the FindSiteMapNode() Method

The FindSiteMapNode() method returns a site map node based on a given URL or GUID. We will create two overloaded versions of the method.

The first accepts a string, which could be a GUID or a URL, and returns a node. To detect whether we are working with a URL or a GUID, we look at the first character of the string. If it begins with an open curly brace ({), then it must surely be a GUID.

From the GUID, we obtain the corresponding channel item using the Searches. GetByGuid() method. For URLs, we call the helper function EnhancedGetByUrl(). It does the same job as Searches.GetByUrl(), but includes several enhancements as we shall see later.

Once we have obtained the channel item, we will construct a site map node object using the GetSiteMapNodeFromChannelItem() method.

```
public override SiteMapNode FindSiteMapNode(string urlOrGuid)
{
    ChannelItem ci = null;
    if (urlOrGuid.StartsWith("{"))
    {
        ci = CmsHttpContext.Current.Searches.GetByGuid(urlOrGuid)
            as ChannelItem;
    }
    else
    {
        ci = EnhancedGetByUrl(CmsHttpContext.Current, urlOrGuid);
    }

    return GetSiteMapNodeFromChannelItem(ci);
}
```

The second method accepts the current HttpContext and returns the node that represents the channel item that is currently being accessed.

```
public override SiteMapNode FindSiteMapNode(HttpContext context)
{
    ChannelItem ci = CmsHttpContext.Current.ChannelItem;
    return GetSiteMapNodeFromChannelItem(ci);
}
```

Enhancing the Searches.GetByUrl() Method

Mapping channel names to host headers is a useful feature found in the Enterprise Edition of MCMS. It enables multiple websites to be hosted on the same server. When enabled, top-level channels directly below the root channel become host headers as well. For example, if the channel directly beneath the root channel is named `tropicalgreen`, the URL of the channel becomes `http://tropicalgreen`, instead of `http://localhost/tropicalgreen`.

The trouble is that the `Searches.GetByUrl()` method does not work reliably when mapped host headers are enabled. When the `Searches.GetByUrl()` method is fed the URL of, say, the top-level channel, `http://tropicalgreen`, we would expect it to return an instance of the `tropicalgreen` channel. However, it returns a null object instead. This is because an issue with the `Searches.GetByUrl()` method causes it to expect the input URL to be `http://localhost/tropicalgreen` regardless of whether or not mapping channel names to host header names is enabled.

As a workaround, we will enhance the `Searches.GetByUrl()` method. We first check to see if the mapped host header feature has been enabled. To do so, we look at the URL of the root channel. If the root channel's URL is `http://Channels/` (the URL contains the name of the root channel itself), we know that channels have been mapped to host headers.

If the map channel names to host header feature has been turned on, we will convert the URL to a path and use the `Searches.GetByPath()` method to get an instance of the channel item. For example, if the URL is `http://tropicalgreen/plantcatalog`, the routine converts it to the channel's path, `/Channels/tropicalgreen/plantcatalog`, and gets an instance of the channel item based on the path. Add the following code to the class:

```
private bool MapChannelToHostHeaderEnabled(CmsContext ctx)
{
    return (ctx.RootChannel.UrlModePublished == "http://Channels/");
}

private ChannelItem EnhancedGetByUrl(CmsContext ctx, string Url)
{
    if (MapChannelToHostHeaderEnabled(ctx))
    {
        string Path = HttpUtility.UrlDecode(Url);
        Path = Path.Replace("http://", "/Channels/");
        if (!Path.StartsWith("/Channels/"))
        {
            Path = "/Channels/" + HttpContext.Current.Request.Url.Host
```

```
            + Path;
        }

        if (Path.EndsWith(".htm"))
        {
            Path = Path.Substring(0, Path.Length - 4);
        }

        if (Path.EndsWith("/"))
        {
            Path = Path.Substring(0, Path.Length - 1);
        }
        return (ChannelItem)(ctx.Searches.GetByPath(Path));
    }
    else
    {
        return ctx.Searches.GetByUrl(Url);
    }
}
```

Implementing the GetParentNode() Method

The GetParentNode() returns the parent node of a specified node. For MCMS, the parent will always be the parent channel of the current channel item. Getting the parent is essentially a two-step process (if you exclude the step about hiding the root channel, of course).

1. Get an instance of the channel item.

2. Use ChannelItem.Parent to get the parent channel of the channel item.

3. Hide the root channel, /Channels/, from the site map.

We start by retrieving the GUID stored in the node's key. With the GUID, we use the Searches.GetByGuid() method to retrieve the corresponding channel item.

```
public override SiteMapNode GetParentNode(SiteMapNode node)
{
    // Get the current channel item
    ChannelItem ci =
            CmsHttpContext.Current.Searches.GetByGuid(node.Key)
            as ChannelItem;
}
```

To get the parent, we simply retrieve the channel returned by the `ChannelItem.` `Parent` property. There's a chance that the current channel item may be null. For example, when the page status is `New`, it doesn't quite exist yet, and although we have its GUID, we can't get an instance of it. In such cases, we will set the parent to be the current channel.

```
public override SiteMapNode GetParentNode(SiteMapNode node)
{
    . . . code continues . . .

    // Variable for storing the parent channel item
    ChannelItem.parent = null;

    if (ci != null)
    {
      if (ci.Path != RootChannel)
      {
        // Get the parent of the current channel item
        parent = ci.Parent;
      }
    }
    else
    {
        // We've got a null channel item, possibly because the
        // page's status is New
        // Set the parent to be the current channel
        parent = CmsHttpContext.Current.Channel;
    }
}
```

Once we have an instance of the parent channel item, we use the `GetSiteMapNodeFromChannelItem()` method to create a site map node from the channel item.

```
public override SiteMapNode GetParentNode(SiteMapNode node)
{
    . . . code continues . . .
    // Create a site map node based on the parent channel item
    // and return it
    return GetSiteMapNodeFromChannelItem(parent);
}
```

The `GetParentNode()` method isn't complete yet. If you run it now, you will find that it returns the root node, `/Channels/`. As a result, controls like the `SiteMapPath` control will display a trail that includes the root channel, `/Channels/`.

It's probably a good idea to hide the root channel from the site map, since it isn't a visible part of the site's hierarchy. There are a couple of situations where the root node may get included in the site map:

- The node being accessed is that of the root channel, /Channels/, itself.
- The node being accessed is a page or channel item located in the root channel. For example, it could be a home page (/Channels/Home.htm) or one of the top-level channels (/Channels/tropicalgreen/). Therefore, its parent is the root channel.

In both situations, we need to set the return value of GetParentNode() to be null in order to hide the root channel in the site map. Add the highlighted code as shown here:

```
public override SiteMapNode GetParentNode(SiteMapNode node)
{
    . . . code continues . . .

    if (parent == null)
    {
        // The parent is null, possibly because we are somehow
        // accessing the root channel itself.
        return null;
    }
    else {
        // Check to see if the parent channel is "/Channels/"
        if(parent.Path == "/Channels/" && RootChannel != "/Channels/")
        {
            // We don't want "Channels" to be part of the site map
            return null;
        }
        else
        {
            // Create a site map node based on the parent channel item
            // and return it
            return GetSiteMapNodeFromChannelItem(parent);
        }
    }
}
```

The completed method looks as follows:

```
public override SiteMapNode GetParentNode(SiteMapNode node)
{
    // Get the current channel item
```

```
ChannelItem ci = CmsHttpContext.Current.Searches.GetByGuid
               (node.Key) as ChannelItem;

// Variable for storing the parent channel item
ChannelItem parent = null;

if (ci != null)
{
    if (ci.Path != RootChannel)
    {
        // Get the parent of the current channel item
        parent = ci.Parent;
    }
}
else
{
    // We've got a null channel item, possibly because the
    // page's status is New
    // Set the parent to be the current channel
    parent = CmsHttpContext.Current.Channel;
}

if (parent == null)
{
    // The parent is null, possibly because we are somehow
    // accessing the root channel itself.
    return null;
}
else
{
    // Check to see if the parent channel is "/Channels/"
    if (parent.Path == "/Channels/" && RootChannel != "/Channels/")
    {
        // We don't want "Channels" to be part of the site map
        return null;
    }
    else
    {
        // Create a site map node based on the parent channel item
        // and return it
```

```
        return GetSiteMapNodeFromChannelItem(parent);
    }
  }
}
```

Implementing the GetChildNodes() Method

The GetChildNodes() method returns a list of all children (sub-channels and postings) of a specified node. As before, we use the GUID stored in the node's key to retrieve the channel. We then loop through the collection of sub-channels and postings and add them to the site map as nodes.

```
public override SiteMapNodeCollection GetChildNodes(SiteMapNode node)
{
    SiteMapNodeCollection smnc = new SiteMapNodeCollection();

    Channel currentChannel =
            CmsHttpContext.Current.Searches.GetByGuid(node.Key)
            as Channel;

    if (currentChannel != null)
    {
        ChannelCollection cc = currentChannel.Channels;
        cc.SortByDisplayName();

        foreach (Channel c in cc)
        {
            smnc.Add(GetSiteMapNodeFromChannelItem(c));
        }

        PostingCollection pc = currentChannel.Postings;
        pc.SortByDisplayName();

        foreach (Posting p in pc)
        {
            smnc.Add(GetSiteMapNodeFromChannelItem(p));
        }
    }

    return smnc;
}
```

Notice that before looping through the sub-channels and postings, we sorted each collection by display name. You could easily change the sort order by calling the other sorting functions such as `SortByStartDate()` or `SortBySortOrdinal()` or implement a custom sort algorithm.

Registering the SiteMapProvider

The `MCMSSiteMapProvider` is complete. Before we can use the `SiteMapProvider`, we need to register it in the `web.config` file. Add the highlighted code between the `<System.Web>` tags as shown here:

```
<system.web>
    . . . code continues . . .


  <siteMap defaultProvider="MCMSSiteMapProvider" enabled="true">
    <providers>
      <add name="MCMSSiteMapProvider"
           type="TropicalGreen.MCMSSiteMapProvider"/>
    </providers>
  </siteMap>
</system.web>
```

The SiteMapPath Control

The `SiteMapPath` control displays a series of hyperlinks that lead back to the home page. It is sometimes known as a breadcrumb trail, as it resembles the trail of bread left behind by the fictitious characters Hansel and Gretel. It's the "You are here" sign that tells visitors to the site where they are. For example, when viewing a plant page, the `SiteMapPath` control displays **Home > Plant Catalog > Aloe Vera**.

Having the `SiteMapPath` control on the page makes it easy for visitors to get back to the plant catalog, or any other parent nodes. As we shall see, it is also fairly simple to include in an MCMS site.

In earlier versions of ASP.NET (version 1.x), we had to write recursive functions to get a collection of parent channels that lead up to the root. With the `SiteMapProvider` that we've created earlier and the `SiteMapPath` control, we can achieve the same result without writing a single line of code. Let's take a look at how it's done.

1. First, open the `TropicalGreen.master` master page created earlier in Chapter 3 (*Using Master Pages*) in Visual Studio.

2. Switch to **Design** view and drag a **SiteMapPath** control from the **Navigation** section of the toolbar and drop it onto the text marker that says **Space for SiteMapPath Control**. Then delete the text marker.

3. Save the file.

We've added the `SiteMapPath` control to the site. To see how it appears on the site, navigate to any page. Notice that the control displays all links that lead up to the site's root channel.

Home > Plant Catalog > Aloe Vera

What's happening behind the scenes is that the `SiteMapProvider` has supplied the `SiteMapPath` control with the parent channels that lead to the current page. Without any extra programming on our part, the two components have worked together to generate the trail.

The Menu Control

The ubiquitous menu control needs little introduction. Menus provide users with a list of links from which to choose. They are traditionally placed either horizontally at the top of the page, or vertically on the left or right-hand side of the page. If you've built a website, chances are you've attempted to put a menu somewhere on the site either by using ready-to-use widgets or by building one entirely from scratch using a collection of scripts. Either way, a fair amount of code had to be written to get the menu working.

Creating menus with the menu control of ASP.NET 2.0 is a breeze. Let's add a couple of menus to the TropicalGreen site. We will start by building a static horizontal menu for the site's banner. Following that, we will attempt to do something a little more complex and build a dynamic vertical menu that displays sub-menus as popouts.

Building a Horizontal Menu

Static menus are easy to build. We could simply hard-code the links in the master page and the job is done. However, when the URLs of links change or when new items are added to the list, a developer is still required to do the deed. Moreover, hard-coding also means that all links are visible to all visitors to the site. Without additional coding, it would be difficult to hide links to restricted sites.

It is therefore preferable for menu items to be dynamically generated even though the menu is static. In previous versions of ASP.NET (version 1.x), we had to write recursive functions to generate each menu item. The good news is that the

`SiteMapProvider` does most of the work for us. All that remains to be done is to hook it up to a menu control using a `SiteMapDataSource` control.

Unlike the `SiteMapPath` control, the menu control requires a `SiteMapDataSource` control to bind data from a SiteMapProvider. Let's take a look at how this is done.

1. With `tropicalgreen.master` opened in **Design** view, drag a **SiteMapDataSource** control from the **Data** section of the toolbox and drop it at the bottom of the web form. Right-click the **SiteMapDataSource** control and give it the following property values:

Property	Value
ID	SiteMapDataSourceTop
SiteMapProvider	MCMSSiteMapProvider

2. Drag a **Menu** control from the **Navigation** section of the toolbox and drop it next to the text marker **Space for Top Menu** of the `tropicalgreen.master` file. A smart tag dialog named **Menu Tasks** appears. Set the **Choose Data Source** field to **SiteMapDataSourceTop** and the **Views** field to **Static**.

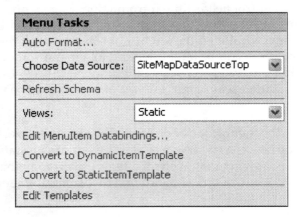

3. Delete the text markers. Give the menu control the following property values:

Property	Value
ID	TopMenu
Orientation	Horizontal
StaticDisplayLevels	2

4. Save the file.

Notice that we have not written a single line of code! To see the horizontal menu in action, view any of the plant pages.

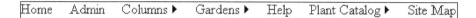

Home   Admin   Columns ▶   Gardens ▶   Help   Plant Catalog ▶   Site Map

The menu appears strange on the first load. All menu items, including sub-menu items that should be hidden are shown. The sub menu items only disappear after the mouse cursor goes over them. What should I do?

The menus require XHTML to display correctly. A `<xhtmlConformance>` tag was added to the `web.config` file when the MCMS web application was created using the wizard. The `<xhtmlConformance>` tag contains an attribute named `mode`, which specifies the XHTML rendering mode for the application. The default `mode` attribute value for MCMS websites is `Legacy`, which means some code will be reverted to conform to the XHTML v1.1 rendering behavior. Change the `mode` attribute value to either `Strict` or `Transitional` for the menu controls to work.

The horizontal menu contains a list of all top-level channel items. However, while showing all items may work on some websites, it won't do for TropicalGreen. We require the horizontal menu to display only three items:

- **Home**
- **Help**
- **Site Map**

Using Custom Properties to Differentiate Between Top and Right Menu Items

To specify the items that appear on the top menu, we have added custom property values to each top-level channel. Each channel has a custom property named `MenuLocation`, which may hold one of two values: `Top` and `Right`. The three channel items, `TropicalGreen`, `Help`, and `SiteMap`, have been configured to have a `MenuLocation` of `Top` as shown in **Site Manager**.

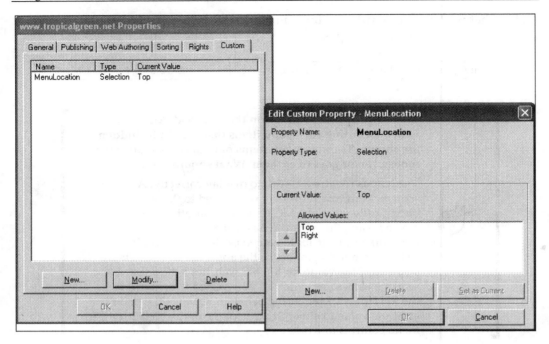

The MCMSSiteMapProviderTop Class

We will need to modify the `SiteMapProvider` to look at the value stored in `MenuLocation`. At the same time, it should continue to display the navigation structure of the entire site for the `SiteMapPath` control added earlier.

Fortunately, ASP.NET 2.0 supports the use of multiple site maps. We could leave the first `SiteMapProvider` intact and create a second one that derives from it. Let's create a second `SiteMapProvider` named `MCMSSiteMapProviderTop`, which only includes channels that have a `MenuLocation` custom property value of `Top`.

1. Add a class file named `MCMSSiteMapProviderTop.cs` to the `\App_Code\ SiteMapProviders` folder.

2. Add the highlighted namespace as well as the namespace declaration.

    ```
    using System;
    using System.Data;
    using System.Configuration;
    using System.Web;
    using System.Web.Security;
    using System.Web.UI;
    using System.Web.UI.WebControls;
    ```

```
using System.Web.UI.WebControls.WebParts;
using System.Web.UI.HtmlControls;
using Microsoft.ContentManagement.Publishing;

namespace TropicalGreen
{
    public class MCMSSiteMapProviderTop
    {
        . . . code continues . . .
    }
}
```

3. We won't attempt to rebuild the `SiteMapProvider` from the ground up. As most of the code has already been written in the `MCMSSiteMapProvider` class we created earlier, we will simply inherit it.

```
public class MCMSSiteMapProviderTop : MCMSSiteMapProvider
{
        . . . code continues . . .
}
```

4. We need to modify the `GetChildNodes()` method to look at the value stored in the `MenuLocation` custom property of each channel. Only channels that belong to the top menu are added to the site map.

```
public override SiteMapNodeCollection GetChildNodes(SiteMapNode
                                                    node)
{
    SiteMapNodeCollection smnc = new SiteMapNodeCollection();

    Channel currentChannel =
            CmsHttpContext.Current.Searches.GetByGuid(node.Key) as
                                                    Channel;

    if (currentChannel != null)
    {
        ChannelCollection cc = currentChannel.Channels;
        cc.SortByDisplayName();

        foreach (Channel c in cc)
        {
            if (c.CustomProperties["MenuLocation"] != null)
            {
                if (c.CustomProperties["MenuLocation"].Value == "Top")
                {
```

```
                        smnc.Add(GetSiteMapNodeFromChannelItem(c));
                }
            }
        }
    }

    return smnc;
}
```

5. The class is complete. Save the file.

6. As before, we need to register `MCMSSiteMapProviderTop` in the `web.config` file before using it. Add the highlighted code to the `web.config` file.

```
<siteMap defaultProvider ="MCMSSiteMapProvider" enabled ="true">
    <providers>
        <add name="MCMSSiteMapProvider"
            type="TropicalGreen.MCMSSiteMapProvider"/>
        <add name="MCMSSiteMapProviderTop"
            type="TropicalGreen.MCMSSiteMapProviderTop"/>
    </providers>
</siteMap>
```

7. To see it in action, set the `SiteMapProvider` property of `SiteMapDataSourceTop` to `MCMSSiteMapProviderTop`.

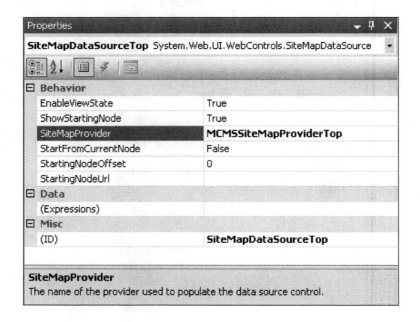

Now navigate to any of the plant pages. The menu shows only the three channel items that we have specified to be at the top.

Home   Help   Site Map

Building a Dynamic Multi-Level Vertical Menu

We've used the menu control to build a single-level static horizontal menu. Now, let's raise the stakes and use the same control to create a multi-level menu. To make things more interesting, we will also rotate the menu ninety degrees and create a vertical display.

All top-level channel items that aren't part of the top menu will be displayed in the vertical menu. When the mouse cursor hovers a parent menu item (e.g. **Gardens**), a popup appears, revealing the list of sub-menu items. Here's what the menu will look like when complete:

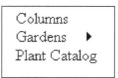

The MCMSSiteMapProviderRight Class

So far, we have created two `SiteMapProvider` classes — the first lists all channel items, and the second contains only top menu items.

Now, let's create a third `SiteMapProvider` class that lists only items for the vertical right menu.

1. Add a class file named `MCMSSiteMapProviderRight.cs` to the `App_Code` folder.

2. The class requires the use of the namespace highlighted in the following code snippet. Add also the namespace declaration.

```
using System;
using System.Data;
using System.Configuration;
using System.Web;
using System.Web.Security;
using System.Web.UI;
using System.Web.UI.WebControls;
using System.Web.UI.WebControls.WebParts;
```

```
using System.Web.UI.HtmlControls;
using Microsoft.ContentManagement.Publishing;

namespace TropicalGreen
{
    public class MCMSSiteMapProviderRight
    {
        . . . code continues . . .
    }
}
```

3. As before, we won't be building the `SiteMapProvider` from scratch. Instead, we will inherit from the `MCMSSiteMapProvider` class that we created earlier.

```
public class MCMSSiteMapProviderRight : MCMSSiteMapProvider
{
    . . . code continues . . .
}
```

4. We will override the `GetChildNodes()` method of the base class and modify it to include only items that belong to the right menu. To do so, we read the value of the custom property `MenuLocation`. If it contains the value `Right`, the item is inserted into the site map. In addition, we will also add sub-menu items to the site map. Append the `GetChildNodes()` method to the code.

```
public override SiteMapNodeCollection GetChildNodes(SiteMapNode
                                                          node)
{
    SiteMapNodeCollection smnc = new SiteMapNodeCollection();

    Channel currentChannel =
            CmsHttpContext.Current.Searches.GetByGuid(node.Key) as
                                              Channel;

    if (currentChannel != null)
    {
        ChannelCollection cc = currentChannel.Channels;
        cc.SortByDisplayName();

        foreach (Channel c in cc)
        {
            if (c.CustomProperties["MenuLocation"] != null)
            {
                // Add top-level menu items
```

```
        if (c.CustomProperties["MenuLocation"].Value == "Right")
        {
        smnc.Add(GetSiteMapNodeFromChannelItem(c));
        }
    }
    else if(c.Parent.Path!=base.RootChannel)
    {
    // Add sub menu items
    smnc.Add(GetSiteMapNodeFromChannelItem(c));
    }
  }
}

return smnc;
}
```

5. The class is complete. Save the file.

6. Before the `MCMSSiteMapProviderRight` class can be used, we need to register it in the `web.config` file.

```
<siteMap defaultProvider ="MCMSSiteMapProvider" enabled ="true">
  <providers>
    <add name="MCMSSiteMapProvider"
        type="TropicalGreen.MCMSSiteMapProvider"/>
    <add name="MCMSSiteMapProviderTop"
        type="TropicalGreen.MCMSSiteMapProviderTop"/>
    <add name="MCMSSiteMapProviderRight"
        type="TropicalGreen.MCMSSiteMapProviderRight"/>
  </providers>
</siteMap>
```

The `SiteMapProviderRight` class has been built and registered. Let's add a `SiteMapDataSource` and menu control to the `tropicalgreen.master` template.

1. With `tropicalgreen.master` opened, drag a **SiteMapDataSource** control from the **Data** section of the toolbox and assign the following property values:

Property	Value
ID	SiteMapDataSourceRight
SiteMapProvider	MCMSSiteMapProviderRight
ShowStartingNode	False

2. Next, drag a menu control from the **Navigation** section of the toolbox and drop it next to the text marker **Space for Right Menu**.

3. The **Menu Tasks** dialog appears. Set the **Choose Data Source** field to **SiteMapDataSourceRight** and the **Views** field to **Static**. Although the right menu is a dynamic menu, we still require the first level to be static, hence the choice of a static view.

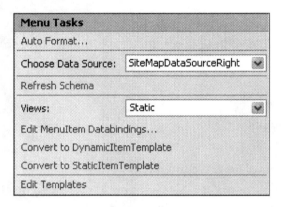

4. Delete the text marker **Space for Right Menu**.

5. Set the following property values for the menu control. Notice that we have set the StaticDisplayLevels property to 1. This means that only the first-level items will be shown as static text. Sub-menu items will be dynamic and revealed as popups.

Property	Value
ID	MenuRight
StaticDisplayLevels	1

The right menu control is complete. To view it, navigate to any of the plant pages on the website. Place the mouse cursor over the **Gardens** menu item to reveal the sub-menu item **Members**.

The TreeView Control

The `TreeView` control provides a hierarchical view of all items on the site. It is often used in site maps or as an alternative to the menu control. TreeViews are popular because they are intuitive to use. Most users would instinctively know how to expand and collapse folders to get content.

Let's add a page that uses the `TreeView` control. We will use it to display a graphical view of the entire site map and link it to the **Site Map** link in the top horizontal menu item. Here's how the completed tree will look when done. Don't worry about the look and feel of the tree for now; we will spice it up with colors and images in the next chapter on themes.

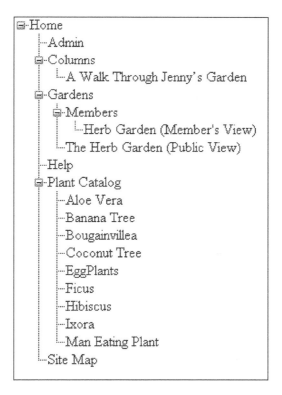

The first cut of our site map loads all nodes into the tree at once. In a later section, we will show how nodes may be populated on demand, when the parent node is expanded.

The Site Map Page

Let's create a channel-rendering script for the SiteMap channel. Users can access the page by clicking on the **Site Map** link on the top horizontal menu bar.

1. Add a web form to the **Templates** folder of the **TropicalGreen** project. Name the web form **SiteMap.aspx**. Choose to **Select a master page** and click **Add**.

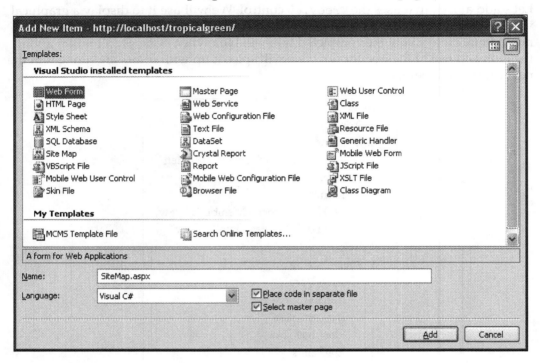

2. In the **Select a Master Page** dialog, choose the Tropicalgreen.master template in the **Templates** folder. Click **OK**.

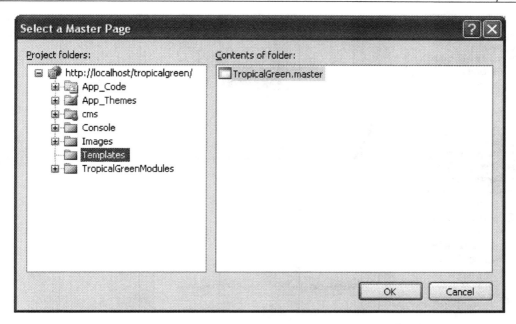

3. Open `Sitemap.aspx` in **Design** view. Drag a **SiteMapDataSource** control from the **Data** section of the toolbox and drop it into the content area. Assign the following property values to the `SiteMapDataSource` control:

Property	Value
ID	SiteMapDataSourceTree
SiteMapProvider	MCMSSiteMapProvider

4. Drag a **TreeView** control from the **Navigation** section of the toolbox into the content area, above the **SiteMapDataSource** control.

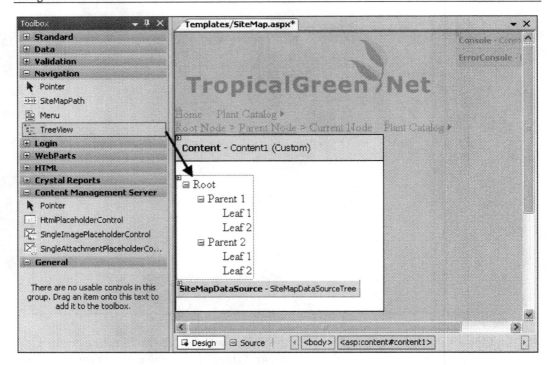

5. As soon as the **TreeView** control has been added to the form, the **TreeView Tasks** dialog appears. Set the **Choose Data Source** field to **SiteMapDataSourceTree** and select the **Show Lines** checkbox.

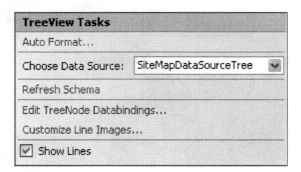

The page is complete. Save and build the website. Now, let's check the properties of the `SiteMap` channel to ensure that it links to the `SiteMap.aspx` page. If you have downloaded the site deployment file from the book's companion website, the `SiteMap` channel will already be configured to display the `SiteMap.aspx` page. Otherwise, take the following steps to set the properties of the `SiteMap` channel.

1. Open **Site Manager** and navigate to the **SiteMap** channel.

2. Right-click on the **SiteMap** channel and select **Properties**.

3. In the **Properties** dialog, click the **Publishing** tab.

4. In the **Channel Rendering** section of the dialog, click **Select**.

5. In the **Select Channel Rendering** dialog, set the **Script URL** field to
   /tropicalgreen/templates/sitemap.aspx and click **OK**.

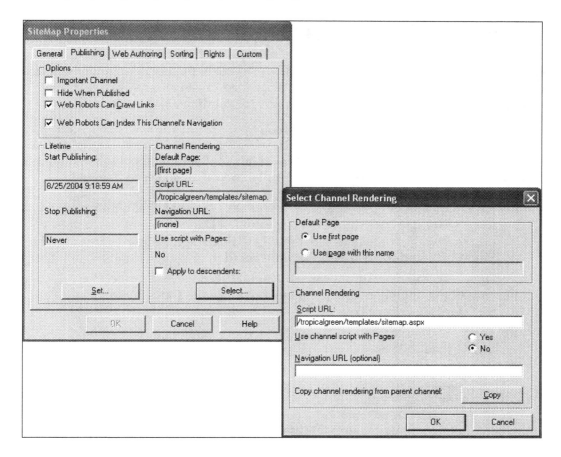

6. Close all open dialogs.

Now navigate to any page on the website and click on the **Site Map** link on the top menu bar. The entire tree is loaded and displayed. Expand or contract any of the nodes to reveal the sub-items.

Here, we have simply dragged and dropped the `TreeView`
control onto the page and added the necessary logic for
building the tree directly onto the page itself. A better
design would be to add the `TreeView` control to a web
user control or a server control. Encapsulated within a web
user control or server control, the site map may be reused
across multiple places in the site.

Populating Nodes on Demand

For very large trees, it may not be practical to populate the entire `TreeView` control
each time it loads. Imagine a site where there are tens of thousands of nodes in a tree;
it may take quite a while before all nodes get loaded. As an alternative, we could
configure the tree to load child nodes only after expanding a parent node.

The good news is, tree view nodes of the `TreeView` control already have a built-in
property named `PopulateOnDemand`, which when set to `true`, will cause child nodes
to be populated only when a parent node expands for the first time. Let's take a look
at how we can configure the `TreeView` control to populate nodes on demand.

1. Open the `Plant.aspx` template file created earlier in **Design** view.

2. Drag a **SiteMapDataSource** control from the **Data** section of the toolbox and
   drop it into the content area. Set the **ID** to **SiteMapDataSourceTree** and the
   SiteMapProvider to **MCMSSiteMapProvider**.

3. Drag a **TreeView** control from the **Navigation** section of the toolbar
   and drop it anywhere on the content areas. Set the **DataSourceID** to
   SiteMapDataSourceTree.

4. Toggle to **Source** view. Between the `<asp:TreeView>` tags, add the
   highlighted code as shown here:

```
<asp:TreeView ID="TreeView1" runat="server"
    DataSourceID="SiteMapDataSourceTree"
    ShowLines="True">
        <DataBindings>
            <asp:TreeNodeBinding PopulateOnDemand="true"
                    TextField="Title"
                    NavigateUrlField="Url"
                    TooltipField="Description"/>
        </DataBindings>
</asp:TreeView>
```

The `<DataBindings>` tag enables us to specify how each site map node
transforms to a tree view node. Here, we have set the `PopulateOnDemand`
property of each tree view node to be `true`. In addition, we have mapped the
following properties between the tree view node and the site map node:

TreeViewNode	SiteMapNode
Text	Title
NavigateUrl	Url
Tooltip	Description

5. Next, we set the depth of the tree such that only the first-level nodes are shown. We will also set the `PopulateNodesFromClient` property of the `TreeView` to `true` so that visitors using the latest browsers (browsers later than Internet Explorer 5.5 or Netscape 6.0) will not have the entire page reloaded when retrieving child nodes. Instead, a set of JavaScripts (also called **AJAX** or **Asynchronous JavaScript and XML**) will be generated. The scripts will make use of Microsoft's XMLHTTP ActiveX object to call server-side scripts and asynchronously load child nodes into the tree without refreshing the entire page.

```
<asp:TreeView ID="TreeView1" runat="server"
   DataSourceID="SiteMapDataSourceTree"
   ShowLines="True" PopulateNodesFromClient="True"
      ExpandDepth="1">
      . . . code continues . . .
</asp:TreeView>
```

We have configured the tree to populate nodes on demand. View any of the plant pages. Notice that the tree now only displays the root channel as well as the first-level items. Expand any node and notice that each time you do so, the script that's being called by the page is `TreeView_PopulateNode()`.

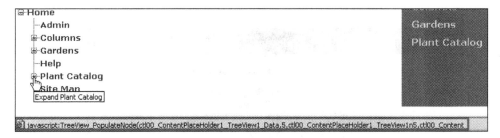

Now place your mouse cursor over the [-] sign. Note that the script that's being called has changed to `TreeView_ToggleNode()`. The change in the name of the function being called indicates that the node did indeed make a round-trip to retrieve the child nodes when it was first expanded.

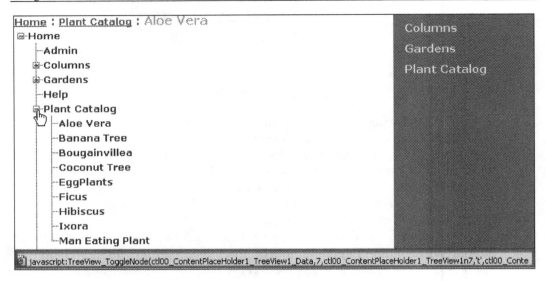

Removing the Leave Warning Message When Expanding Nodes in Edit Mode

There's a problem with the `TreeView` control when it's displayed in a posting in edit mode. Each time a node is expanded, the leave warning message appears.

Refresh the page by pressing *F5* so that the tree collapses to its original state. Now switch to edit site and edit the posting. Expand any of the tree's nodes. Did you receive a message warning you that by refreshing the page you will lose any unsaved changes?

The leave warning alert was designed to appear when the browser's `OnBeforeUnload()` event is fired. Usually, this happens when the browser window closes or when the page navigates to a different location. If you view the HTML source of the page (right-click anywhere on the page and choose **View Source**), you will find that the `TreeView_PopulateNode()` method is triggered by the anchor's `href` attribute:

```
<a id="ctl00_ContentPlaceHolder1_TreeView1n2" href="javascript:
TreeView_PopulateNode(. . . code continues . . .)">
```

Using the anchor's `href` attribute gets the job done, but it does cause the page to unload, hence prompting the leave warning message to appear.

Instead of using the anchor's `href` attribute to call the script, we should instead use the `onclick()` method. The `onclick()` event behaves like a regular **Submit** button. The page's URL does not change when it fires, and therefore does not trigger the page's `OnBeforeUnload()` event, and the alert does not appear.

We need to move the entire content of the anchor's `href` attribute and embed it in the `onclick()` event such that the generated code appears as follows. The script should return `false` so as to cancel any further action that may be taking place, such as the execution of the `href` attribute.

```
<a id="ctl00_ContentPlaceHolder1_TreeView1n2"
onclick="TreeView_PopulateNode(. . . code continues . . .);
                            return false;">
```

The best way to go about modifying the way the anchor tag is generated is to create a custom `TreeView` control and override its `Render()` method.

1. Add a C# Class Library project to the solution. Name the project **TropicalGreenControlLib**.

2. Delete the `Class1.cs` file generated by the wizard. We won't need it.

3. Add a reference to the `System.Web` library to the project.

4. Add a class file named `MCMSTreeView.cs` to the project.

5. The code requires the use of the methods in the namespaces highlighted in the following snippet. Add them above the namespace declaration.

```
. . . code continues . . .
using System.Web;
using System.Web.UI;
using System.Web.UI.WebControls;
using System.IO;
using System.Text.RegularExpressions;

namespace TropicalGreenControlLib
{
    . . . code continues . . .
}
```

6. As we are merely modifying the way the tree view is rendered, we won't attempt to build the control from scratch. Instead, have the custom control inherit from the `System.Web.UI.WebControls.TreeView` class.

```
public class MCMSTreeView : TreeView
{
}
```

7 To modify the anchors generated by the base `TreeView` class, we need to override the `Render()` method. We first retrieve the HTML output generated by the base `TreeView` control. Once we have gotten the original content, we look for instances of the `href` attribute. Using a regular expression, we get the value that was previously stored in the `href` attribute and move it to the `onclick()` event handler of the anchor. Add the code as shown here:

```
protected override void Render(System.Web.UI.HtmlTextWriter
                               output)
{
    // Get the output of the original TreeView Control
    TextWriter tempWriter = new StringWriter();
    base.Render(new System.Web.UI.HtmlTextWriter(tempWriter));
    string orightml = tempWriter.ToString();

    // Search for the javascript postback code in the href attribute
    // and if found add an onclick event handler to execute it in a
    // way that does not cause the MCMS authoring warning to show up
    Regex hrefRegex =
            new Regex("href=\"javascript:(?<PostBackScript>.*?)\"",
                    RegexOptions.Singleline);
    string newhtml = hrefRegex.Replace(orightml,
                    "href=\"javascript:${PostBackScript}\" " +
                    "onclick=\"eval(this.href.substr(11)); " +
                    "return false;\"");
    output.Write(newhtml);
}
```

8. The control is complete. Save and compile the **TropicalGreenControlLib** project.

To use the custom control, add it to the **Toolbox** by right-clicking anywhere within the box and by selecting **Choose Items**. In the **Choose Items** dialog, select the **.NET Framework Components** tab. Click on the **Browse** button and select the `TropicalGreenControlLib.dll` file found in the `/debug/bin/` folder of the **TropicalGreenControlLib** project.

Once the control has been added to the toolbox, drag and drop it anywhere onto the editable areas of the `Plant.aspx` template file. Set the properties of the `MCMSTreeview` as we did for the `TreeView` control earlier. When rendered on a page, the nodes expand and collapse as you would expect them to, and the leave warning message does not appear even in edit mode.

When you are done, delete all `TreeView` controls from the plant template file.

Getting the Populate-On-Demand Feature of the TreeView Control to Work in Channel-Rendering Scripts

As we have seen, the populate-on-demand feature works when embedded within a template file. However, if you attempted to add it to a channel-rendering script, you may have found that the `TreeView` control appears to freeze when you expand any node. As an example, let's modify the `TreeView` control of the `SiteMap.aspx` page created earlier:

1. Open `SiteMap.aspx` file in **Source** view.

2. Modify the properties of the **TreeView** control as shown here:

```
<asp:TreeView ID="TreeView1" runat="server" DataSourceID=
                                      "SiteMapDataSourceTree"
ShowLines="True" PopulateNodesFromClient="True" ExpandDepth="1">
    <DataBindings>
        <asp:TreeNodeBinding PopulateOnDemand="true"
            TextField="Title"
            NavigateUrlField="Url"
            TooltipField="Description"/>
    </DataBindings>
</asp:TreeView>
```

3. Save the page.

When you are done, navigate to the **Site Map** page. Attempt to expand any of the nodes. Notice that nothing happens!

To understand why this happens, let's take a close look at the way the populate-on-demand feature works. When a node is expanded, a postback is performed silently by the browser. The postback requires the information stored in the `action` attribute of the `<form>` tag. If you looked at the generated HTML of the page, you would find that the value stored in the `action` attribute of the `form` resembles the following:

```
<form name="aspnetForm" method="post" action="sitemap.aspx?...code
continues...>
```

What's interesting about the value stored in the `action` attribute is that it's a relative URL. In regular web applications, using a relative URL works well. However, for MCMS pages, the URL has to be absolute. That's because the URL used to access the page (e.g. `http://tropicalgreen/sitemap/`) does not lead to a physical folder—it's purely virtual and points to a channel in the repository. So when it tries to access the relative URL such as `sitemap.aspx`, it looks for it at `http://tropicalgreen/sitemap/sitemap.aspx`. Because the file does not physically exist at that location, the code fails.

To correct this problem, we need to use absolute links instead. To generate an absolute link in the `action` attribute of the form, we can choose to:

1. Generate a `<base>` tag and store the absolute path to the page there. With a `<base>` tag, all relative links are converted to absolute links by prepending the value stored in the tag to the link. Usually, the `<base>` tag gets generated by the `RobotMetaTag` control. However, a bug in the control prevents it from generating the `<base>` tag in a channel-rendering script. An enhanced version of the `RobotMetaTag` that works on both channel-rendering scripts and template files can be found here: `http://www.gotdotnet.com/Community/UserSamples/Details.aspx?SampleGuid=8600bae5-7aba-481b-93bb-d179927179d5`.

2. Modify the `action` attribute of the `<form>` tag using client-side JavaScripts. While generating the `<base>` tag is a possible solution, you may not want to enable it (we discuss some possible reasons why `<base>` tags can't be used, in Chapter 5). For this method to work, we need to modify the way the tree view is rendered, and to do so, we will have to create a custom `TreeView` control. Since we have already created a custom `TreeView` control earlier, let's explore how we can enhance it to work in a channel-rendering script.

The populate-on-demand feature of the `TreeView` control worked for the plant template file because we have set the `RenderBaseHref` property of the `RobotMetaTag` control to `true`. If it had been set to `false`, the `<base>` tag would not be generated, and the tree view would not have been able to populate child nodes on demand.

We need to convert the relative link stored in the `action` attribute of the form to an absolute link. To do so, we will leverage some of the existing functionality found in the generated page.

If you examined the HTML source of any MCMS page, you would find a JavaScript variable named __CMS_PostbackForm, which stores an instance of the form object.

```
var __CMS_PostbackForm = document.forms['aspnetForm'];
```

In addition, there is a variable named __CMS_CurrentUrl that stores the absolute URL of the page. Here's how the __CMS_CurrentUrl of the **Site Map** page may look on your page. Note that the GUID values on your site may be different.

```
var __CMS_CurrentUrl = "/tropicalgreen/templates/sitemap.aspx?
    NRMODE=Published&
    NRNODEGUID=%7b6E3510D2-519A-4D4F-92A8-621B43F5894F%7d&
    NRORIGINALURL=%2ftropicalgreen%2fSiteMap%2f&
    NRCACHEHINT=ModifyLoggedIn";
```

Putting the pieces together, in order to assign the value stored in __CMS_CurrentUrl to the value of the action attribute of the form, __CMS_PostbackForm, we need to somehow execute the following script on the client:

```
<script type="text/javascript">
    if (typeof (__CMS_CurrentUrl) != "undefined")
    {
        __CMS_PostbackForm.action = __CMS_CurrentUrl;
    }
</script>
```

A good place to register the script is in the Render() method of the TreeView control. Open the MCMSTreeView.cs file and add the highlighted code to the Render() method.

```
protected override void Render(System.Web.UI.HtmlTextWriter output)
{
    . . . code continues . . .

    // Register a client script that ensures that the action property
    // is correct when AJAX tries to do its postback.
    string script = "\n<script type=\"text/javascript\">\n" +
            "    if (typeof (__CMS_CurrentUrl) != " +
            " \"undefined\")\n" +
            "    {\n" +
            "        __CMS_PostbackForm.action = " +
            "__CMS_CurrentUrl;\n" +
            "    }\n" +
            "</script>\n";
```

```
Page.ClientScript.RegisterStartupScript(this.GetType(),
    "AdjustActionForTreeView", script);
}
```

Now, replace the `TreeView` control on `SiteMap.aspx` with the custom `MCMSTreeView` control. After setting it up to populate nodes on demand, the tree no longer freezes, and you should be able to expand and contract nodes to reveal sub-nodes.

Using the TreeView Control in Summary Pages

Summary pages (also known as default, cover, or index pages) provide a listing of pages within a given section. They are particularly useful when visitors know only of the existence of a page but not it's exact location. For example, you may know that there's a page that describes the Aloe Vera in the plant catalog, but you may not know its address. If the plant catalog page provides a listing of all the plant pages on the site, you could easily find the page that you are looking for.

Early versions of summary pages were often hand-coded pieces of work that had to be updated frequently when new pages were added, deleted, or renamed. Over the years, this practice has slowly been phased out when active-scripting enabled developers to dynamically assemble the summary page on the fly. This meant that the page showed the latest version of the list, providing for efficient and effective link management.

In MCMS sites built on ASP.NET 1.x, summary pages were typically built by iterating through the collection of channels and postings. The collection of channel items was then displayed in a table-like control such as the DataGrid. While this technique still works today, ASP.NET 2.0 introduces a faster and easier approach to building summary pages.

Let's take a look at an alternative solution that involves building a custom site-map provider and the `TreeView` control. Here's the game plan:

1. We start off by creating a custom site-map provider that sets the currently viewed channel as the root node. All postings within the channel are then added as site-map nodes.

2. Next, we will use the `TreeView` control to provide a listing of all pages within the channel. While the `TreeView` control is designed to show a hierarchical listing of items, its versatility allows it to display a simple single-level list just as well.

When completed, the summary for the plant catalog channel will resemble this:

- Aloe Vera
- Banana Tree
- Bougainvillea
- Coconut Tree
- EggPlants
- Ficus
- Hibiscus
- Ixora
- Man Eating Plant

The SiteMapProviderSummary Class

Let's start by creating the custom site-map provider class, which will be similar to the `MCMSSiteMapProvider` class created earlier, with a couple of differences: Instead of containing a hierarchical list of all channels on the site, the site map will start from (and contain only) the currently viewed channel. Secondly, only pages within the current channel will be added to the site map.

1. Add a class file to the `App_Code/SiteMapProviders` folder of the **TropicalGreen** project. Name the file **MCMSSiteMapProviderSummary.cs**.

2. We will need to make use of methods in the namespace highlighted in the following code. Add the highlighted namespace as well as the namespace declaration.

```
using System;
using System.Data;
using System.Configuration;
using System.Web;
using System.Web.Security;
using System.Web.UI;
using System.Web.UI.WebControls;
using System.Web.UI.WebControls.WebParts;
using System.Web.UI.HtmlControls;
using Microsoft.ContentManagement.Publishing;

namespace TropicalGreen
{
    . . . code continues . . .
}
```

3. As with the other custom site-map providers that we have built, we won't write this one from scratch. We will take the short-cut and inherit from the `MCMSSiteMapProvider` class that we created earlier.

```
public class MCMSSiteMapProviderSummary : MCMSSiteMapProvider
{
        . . . code continues . . .
}
```

4. Since the list shows the contents of a single channel, we don't need to add all other channels to the site map. Instead, we shall set the currently viewed channel as the root site map node path. To do so, we override the `GetRootNodeCore()` method.

```
protected override SiteMapNode GetRootNodeCore()
{
    // Set the currently viewed channel to be the root node
    Channel root = CmsHttpContext.Current.Channel;
    return base.GetSiteMapNodeFromChannelItem(root);
}
```

5. Next, we will override the `GetChildNodes()` method. We retrieve a collection of all pages within the current channel and sort them alphabetically by display name. We will then add them one by one to the site map.

```
public override SiteMapNodeCollection GetChildNodes(SiteMapNode
                                                    node)
{
    // Create a new SiteMapNodeCollection
    SiteMapNodeCollection smnc = new SiteMapNodeCollection();

    // Get an instance of the currently viewed channel
    Channel channel =
        CmsHttpContext.Current.Searches.GetByGuid(node.Key) as
                                                        Channel;

    if (channel != null)
    {
        // Get a collection of all postings within the channel
        PostingCollection pc = channel.Postings;

        // Sort the postings by Display Name (from A-Z)
        pc.SortByDisplayName();
```

```
        // Add each posting to the site map
        foreach (Posting p in pc)
        {
            smnc.Add(GetSiteMapNodeFromChannelItem(p));
        }
    }
    return smnc;
}
```

6. The class is complete. Save the `MCMSSiteMapProviderSummary` class file.

7. As before, we need to add a reference to the custom site-map provider in the `web.config` file before we can use it. Add the highlighted line to the `<providers>` section of the `web.config` file.

```
<providers>
    . . . code continues . . .
  <add name="MCMSSiteMapProviderSummary"
    type="TropicalGreen.MCMSSiteMapProviderSummary"/>
</providers>
```

Configuring the TreeView Control to Display a Flat Listing of Items

Now that we have created the custom site-map provider that provides a listing of all pages within a given channel, we need to find a control that is capable of displaying the list. Out of the box, we have a choice of using either the `SiteMapPath`, `Menu`, or `TreeView` controls. For the purpose of this example, let's pick the `TreeView` control.

It may seem counterintuitive to use the `TreeView` control to display a flat listing of items. After all, it was designed to show a hierarchical list. Nevertheless, we shall see that the `TreeView` control is a very versatile control, able to display hierarchical nested items as well as a single-dimension flat list.

1. First, create a new web form in the `/Templates/` folder of the **TropicalGreen** project. Name the file **ChannelRenderingScript.aspx**. Choose to select a master page.

2. In the **Select a Master Page** dialog, choose the `tropicalgreen.master` file located in the **Templates** folder.

3. With `ChannelRenderingScript.aspx` opened in **Design** view, drag a **SiteMapDataSource** control from the **Data** section of the toolbox and drop it anywhere in the content area. Give the control the following property values:

Property	Value
ID	SiteMapDataSourceSummary
SiteMapProvider	MCMSSiteMapProviderSummary
ShowStartingNode	False

We have set the `SiteMapDataSource` to link to the site map provider that we built earlier: `MCMSSiteMapProviderSummary`. Note that as we don't want the currently viewed channel to be displayed as part of the list, we have set the `ShowStartingNode` property to `false`.

4. Next, drag a **TreeView** control from the **Navigation** section of the toolbox and drop it anywhere in the content area. Give it the following property values:

Property	Value
ID	TreeView1
DataSourceID	SiteMapDataSourceSummary
MaxDataBindDepth	1
ShowExpandCollapse	False

By setting the `MaxDataBindDepth` property to `1`, we have ensured that the `TreeView` control will never show more than one level of items. In this way, the list will always be flat. Also, we set `ShowExpandCollapse` to `false` to prevent the expandable plus [+] and minus [-] signs from appearing.

5. Finally, to display a bullet next to each item on the list, we will manually define the binding of each node. Toggle to **Source** view and add the highlighted code between the `<asp:TreeView>` tags.

```
<asp:TreeView ID="TreeView1" runat="server" DataSourceID=
                                      "SiteMapDataSourceSummary"
    MaxDataBindDepth="1" ShowExpandCollapse="False">
    <DataBindings>
        <asp:TreeNodeBinding TextField="Title" NavigateUrlField="Url"
            ToolTipField="Description" FormatString='<li>{0}'/>
    </DataBindings>
</asp:TreeView>
```

We have bound the tree view node to the `Title`, `Url`, and `Description` properties of the site-map node. In addition, by setting the `FormatString` to include the `<li>` tag, we have included a bullet to be printed next to each item.

6. The page is completed. Save and compile the website.

Next, let's assign the `ChannelRenderingScript.aspx` file to be the channel-rendering script for the plant catalog channel.

1. In **Site Manager**, right-click on the **PlantCatalog** channel. Select **Properties**.
2. In the **PlantCatalog Properties** dialog, click on the **Publishing** tab.
3. In the **Channel Rendering** section, click on the **Select** button.
4. In the **Select Channel Rendering** dialog, enter **/tropicalgreen/templates/ ChannelRenderingScript.aspx** in the **Script URL** field.
5. Click **OK** and close all opened dialogs.

With that, we are ready to view the summary page. Navigate to `http://tropicalgreen/plantcatalog` and view the listing of all plant pages within the channel.

The channel-rendering script, `ChannelRenderingScript.aspx`, can be applied on all other channels on the website. Go ahead and assign it to be the channel-rendering script for the `Columns` and `Gardens` channels as well.

Summary

With the navigation controls that ship with ASP.NET 2.0, building site navigation has never been easier. In this chapter we started by building a custom `SiteMapProvider` that reads off the MCMS repository to populate a site map. Next, we showed how a `SiteMapPath` control works with the custom `SiteMapProvider` to provide a breadcrumb trail of links that show the user exactly where he or she is in the site. We saw that no extra programming was required for the `SiteMapPath` control to work correctly. Following which, we looked at the `Menu` control. We built two versions of the control—a static horizontal menu placed at the top of the page, and a dynamic vertical menu located on the right-hand side of the page. Finally, we demonstrated how the `TreeView` control could be used together with the `SiteMapProvider` to provide a comprehensive view of the site's hierarchy. We showed how it can be configured to populate nodes on demand as well as part of a channel-rendering script to display a summary listing of all postings within a particular channel.

5
Applying Themes

Most websites are designed with a common look and feel in mind. After all, if you went to a site that had pages that are distinctively different from one another, you might start to wonder (probably after the second page) if you were still surfing the same website.

In this chapter, we will see how a common look and feel can be applied efficiently to an MCMS site by using themes. We will create skins and cascading style sheets and demonstrate how they work together to define the appearance of a site. Finally, we will discuss an essential customization required for themes to work correctly in an MCMS site.

Themes versus Cascading Style Sheets

The challenge of maintaining a consistent look and feel across a website is not a new one. Not too long ago, developers used cascading style sheets (CSS) to define how the site should look. The use of CSS was a step towards separating design elements from HTML. Graphic designers could work independently on the CSS file, providing information such as color schemes, font types, spacing, margins, and other visual effects. Should the need arise to change any of these attributes, all that the designer needed to do was to amend the CSS file, and voilà, the look and feel of the site would be instantly refreshed!

Nevertheless, despite the advantages of using CSS, modifications to a site's design still required a fair bit of work. Just think about the last time a complex control such as a new calendar control was introduced to a site that you worked on. In order to give a desired look and feel to the control, several styles had to be applied: One for the title, another for the selected date, and a couple more for the navigation arrows. Also, the same task had to be repeated for each calendar control on the site. You could wrap the "styled" calendar in a custom control and reuse it across the site, but that would mean writing code with design elements in mind, which makes for a complicated work arrangement between developers and designers. In addition, CSS was limited to defining the appearance of controls. For example, you couldn't use it to define the columns that make up a grid or the nodes of a tree.

Another limitation of CSS was the varying levels of support the different browsers had for style sheets. The situation gets more complex when older browsers or alternative web devices such as personal digital assistants and mobile phones are added to the picture. For a website to appear consistent across all browser types and versions, complicated workarounds had to be implemented.

ASP.NET 2.0 takes the idea behind CSS a step further by introducing the concept of themes. A theme acts as a central location for storing information about the site's design. You could store CSS files in a theme. ASP.NET automatically generates links to all CSS files for all pages that reference the theme.

Besides managing CSS files, themes also store entire sets of images and other design files required by the site. In addition, you could define multiple themes within a single site. If you switched the site's theme, the site will automatically pick up the images and other supporting files used by the selected theme. In this way, you could customize the look and feel of a site for various devices or browsers.

Themes may also contain skins. Think of skins as an outer covering of server controls—somewhat like a pillow case. When you slip a new casing over a pillow, you change its design but underneath, the pillow remains essentially the same. In the same way, skins can be applied to ASP.NET server controls. Skins address the design requirements of complex server controls by combining the style definitions of entire controls into a single file as opposed to having multiple style sheets. With skins, you could apply styles and set the properties of complex controls such as Calendars and DataGrids with minimal effort. You could even define elements such as the columns that make up the grid or the nodes of a tree within a skin—a task that was not possible with CSS.

Another nice aspect of themes is that they reside in the web application's directory. You could have multiple web applications, each with its own unique themes. In this way, you could go ahead and apply a theme to postings and not worry about affecting the look and feel of say, pages in other web applications like the MCMS dialogs.

Creating a Theme

Let's start by creating a theme for the TropicalGreen site. We will name the theme **Sunny** and use it to apply a new design on our website. In ASP.NET 2.0, themes used by a single project are stored directly below the project's application folder in a special folder named App_Themes. You can create as many themes (or sub folders) as your site requires.

1. First, let's create the `App_Themes` folder. In **Solution Explorer**, right-click the **TropicalGreen** project and select **Add ASP.NET folder | Theme**. A new folder named `App_Themes` appears.

2. Within the `App_Themes` folder is a subfolder named `Theme1`. Rename the folder to `Sunny`.

Applying a Theme to the Entire Site

We have created a theme named `Sunny`. Now let's apply it to the TropicalGreen site.

In the `web.config` file, look for the `<pages>` tag and add an attribute named `theme` and set its value to `Sunny`.

```
<pages validateRequest="false"
       theme="Sunny"/>
```

We have applied the `Sunny` theme to the TropicalGreen site. However, the theme doesn't define any styles or designs yet. In the next section, we will add skins and style sheets to define the look and feel of the site.

Instead of applying the theme to the entire site, we could have defined it at the page level by setting the `theme` attribute of the `@Page` directive. If we needed more flexibility (for example, when changing the theme based on a user's profile), we could apply the theme using code.

Skins for Server Controls

As the name suggests, skins serve as outer covers of controls. Most out-of-the box ASP.NET server controls support skins. Nevertheless, it's always a good idea to check if the control you plan to work with can be skinned. To do so, look for the `SkinID` property. If the control has a `SkinID` property, you can apply a skin to it.

There are two types of skins:

- **Default skins**, which are applied to all controls that do not have a corresponding skin defined in the `SkinID`. For example, if you define a default skin for a `TextBox` control, all `TextBox` controls on pages that adopt the theme will follow the styles defined in the default skin.

- **Name-controlled skins**, which target only controls that share the same `SkinID`. For instance, you may have a skin for a `TextBox` defined. Suppose the skin has the `SkinID` of `MyTextBox`. Only `TextBox` controls that have a matching `SkinID` of `MyTextBox` will have the skin applied.

Creating a Default Skin

Consider the case of the `SiteMapPath` control created earlier in our `TropicalGreen.master` template. We would like the control to use a colon character (`:`) as the node separator. The font type should be Verdana. All nodes will be in bold font and green color, with the exception of the current node, which will be colored orange. If we set these properties using code, here's how it would look:

```
<asp:SiteMapPath ID="SiteMapPath1" runat="server" Font-Names="Verdana"
PathSeparator=":">
    <PathSeparatorStyle Font-Bold="True" ForeColor="green"/>
    <CurrentNodeStyle ForeColor="orange"/>
    <NodeStyle Font-Bold="True" ForeColor="green"/>
    <RootNodeStyle Font-Bold="True" ForeColor="green"/>
</asp:SiteMapPath>
```

While setting the controls of a property is easily done through code, we can do the same thing using a skin. Before doing so, remove all style properties from the `SiteMapPath` control such that the code becomes:

```
<asp:SiteMapPath ID="SiteMapPath1" runat="server">
</asp:SiteMapPath>
```

Now let's build a skin for the `SiteMapPath` control.

1. In **Solution Explorer**, right-click the **Sunny** folder and select **Add New Item...**
2. In the **Add New Item** dialog, choose to create a new **Skin File** and give it the name **Sunny.skin**.

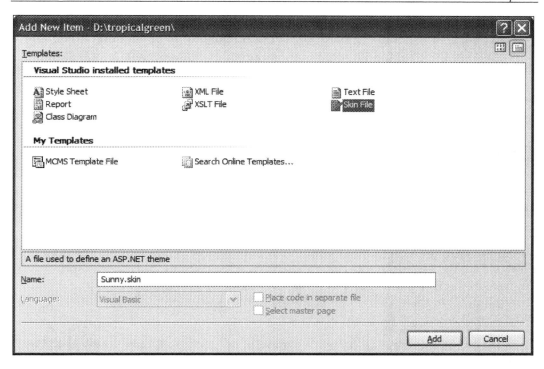

3. The skin file contains sample code that shows how a skin template looks. We won't need the sample for our example. Delete all existing code.

4. Now let's define a skin for the `SiteMapPath` control. For a dramatic effect so that we can see the difference in the screenshots later, we will set the font size to be extra large. Enter the following code in the skin file:

```
<asp:SiteMapPath runat="server" Font-Names="Verdana" Font-Size=
                                 "X-Large" PathSeparator=":">
    <PathSeparatorStyle Font-Bold="True" ForeColor="green"/>
    <CurrentNodeStyle ForeColor="orange"/>
    <NodeStyle Font-Bold="True" ForeColor="green"/>
    <RootNodeStyle Font-Bold="True" ForeColor="green"/>
</asp:SiteMapPath>
```

The code does not look very different from that in specified the original control. The difference is that the code now sits in a skin file instead of being embedded within the template file, providing a clean separation of design and application!

Since the skin that we have created is a default skin, we don't need to do anything more to see it in action. All `SiteMapPath` controls on the TropicalGreen site will immediately adopt the style provided by the skin. Navigate to any page on the website. The nodes of the breadcrumb trail now show up with bold green Verdana font, with the exception of the current node, which is orange, with extra large fonts as defined in the skin.

Home : Plant Catalog : Aloe Vera

Creating a Name-Controlled Skin

What happens when there are controls on the page that should not adopt the default skin? For example, in the SiteMapPath control skinned earlier, we set the default skin to display extra-large sized fonts. If we didn't want to change the default skin, and yet apply a different font setting, we could use **name-controlled skins**.

A name-controlled skin makes use of the SkinID property. Here's how it works. First, we set the SkinID of the control defined in the skin file. Next, we identify the controls in the web form that will adopt that particular skin and set the SkinID of those controls to match the value of the skin. In this way, only controls with the same SkinID will adopt the look and feel of the skin.

Let's try giving the site map control a skin with normal sized fonts. Append a skin control in the Sunny.skin file as follows. Notice that we have set the font size to be Medium and the SkinID to Breadcrumb.

```
<asp:SiteMapPath runat="server" Font-Names="Verdana"
      PathSeparator=":"
      Font-Size="Medium" SkinID="Breadcrumb">
   <PathSeparatorStyle Font-Bold="True" ForeColor="green"/>
   <CurrentNodeStyle ForeColor="orange"/>
   <NodeStyle Font-Bold="True" ForeColor="green"/>
   <RootNodeStyle Font-Bold="True" ForeColor="green"/>
</asp:SiteMapPath>
```

In order for the site map control to pick up the name-controlled skin, we need to assign the SkinID of the control to Breadcrumb as well. In the tropicalgreen.master file, set the SkinID of the control as shown:

```
<asp:SiteMapPath ID="SiteMapPath1" runat="server" SkinID="Breadcrumb">
</asp:SiteMapPath>
```

Save the file. Now, navigate to any of the existing plant postings. The font-size is back to normal, showing that the control now adopts the name-controlled skin instead of the default skin.

Home : Plant Catalog : Aloe Vera

Completing the Skin

Let's complete the skin file by defining skins for both the top horizontal menu and right vertical menu.

First, with `Tropicalgreen.master` open, remove some of the style elements added to the top menu earlier such that the code looks as follows:

```
<asp:Menu ID="Menu1" runat="server" DataSourceID="SiteMapDataSourceTop"
SkinID="TopMenu">
</asp:Menu>
```

We will also remove any style elements that may have been added to the right menu. The code for the right menu should resemble the following:

```
<asp:Menu ID="Menu2" runat="server" DataSourceID=
"SiteMapDataSourceRight" SkinID="RightMenu">
</asp:Menu>
```

Now let's add these style elements back using skins. Add the following skin definitions to the `Sunny.skin` file.

```
<asp:Menu SkinID="TopMenu" runat="server" Orientation="Horizontal"
        MaximumDynamicDisplayLevels="1" StaticDisplayLevels="2"
        StaticMenuItemStyle-CssClass="TopMenu"
        StaticEnableDefaultPopOutImage="False">
</asp:Menu>

<asp:Menu SkinID="RightMenu" runat="server" Orientation="Vertical"
        MaximumDynamicDisplayLevels="1" StaticDisplayLevels="1"
        StaticMenuItemStyle-CssClass="RightMenu"
        StaticEnableDefaultPopOutImage="False">
</asp:Menu>
```

We have added skin definitions for both menus; now set the `SkinID` of the menus to match those of the skins:

Control ID	Set the SkinID to
MenuTop	TopMenu
MenuRight	RightMenu

Notice that the skin definitions make use of cascading style sheets (see the `CssClass` property). We have not created any style sheets yet; so if you took a look at any themed page, you probably wouldn't see much difference after applying the new skin. Let's take a look at how skins and style sheets work together within a theme.

Using Style Sheets

We have seen how skins can be used to apply specific styles on ASP.NET server controls. They are really useful for styling elements such as navigation, form, and other server-side-based controls. Without a doubt, they are pretty nifty and practical tools to have in our toolbox.

However, in the world of MCMS, an important aspect of ensuring that the site has a consistent look and feel throughout is to make sure that content entered by authors in placeholder controls, like the `HtmlPlaceholderControl`, also follows the style guidelines of the website. In order to enforce design rules of HTML content, skins do not help us very much. For HTML controls and code, we still have to make use of good old cascading style sheets.

Previously, to apply a CSS file to a site, we would add a `<link>` tag to all template files and web forms that required it:

```
<link type="text/css" href="UrlOfFile.css"/>
```

Or, we could embed styles directly within the page itself, using `<style>` tags:

```
<style>
H1{color:#993300;font-weight:bold;font-size:14pt}
</style>
```

Either technique will work, but still can be a messy affair especially when working with multiple style sheets and web forms.

The good news is: themes support CSS as well. Now, we can add the CSS file directly to the theme. Behind the scenes, ASP.NET will generate the `<link>` tag for us.

Creating a Style Sheet

The master template of the TropicalGreen site is made up mostly of tables. In addition, all custom content entered by authors is limited to regular HTML text. As these aren't ASP.NET server controls, they do not support skins. To ensure that the look and feel of such content is consistent with the rest of the site, we need to apply a style sheet.

Let's try adding styling to the rest of the TropicalGreen site by using style sheets.

1. To add a style sheet to a theme, right-click on the **Sunny** theme folder in **Solution Explorer** and select **Add New Item...**

2. In the **Add New Item** dialog, choose the **Style Sheet** template and name the file **Sunny.css**.

3. The style sheet that we will use in this example is a relatively simple one. We will specify styles for the body, anchor, and a couple of header levels, as well as a few named styles for the banner and menus. Enter the following code:

```
Body {font-family:Verdana,Arial;font-size:11pt}
A{color:#0000FF;font-size:10pt;font-weight:bold}
H1{color:#993300;font-weight:bold;font-size:14pt}
H2{color:#FF6600;font-weight:bold;font-size:12pt}
.Banner{background-color:#ffcc00}
.TopMenu{background-color:#66cc33;font-weight:bold;color:#CCFF99;
        text-decoration:none;padding:5px;}
.RightMenu{background-color:#669900;color:#CCFF99;
        text-decoration: none;  font-weight:bold;padding:5px;}
```

10. Save `Sunny.css`.

We won't go into the details of the syntax of CSS. For a primer on CSS, take a look at the following website: `http://www.w3c.rl.ac.uk/primers/css/cssprimer.htm`.

Visual Studio also ships with a **Style Builder** that provides a graphical interface for defining styles. To launch the **Style Builder**, toggle to **Design** view and select **Format | Style** from the menu.

Now, take a look at any existing plant posting on the TropicalGreen website. The styles have been successfully applied on the posting.

Why Themes with Style Sheets May Not Work on MCMS Sites

Look at the HTML source of the posting (right-click anywhere on the page and select **View Source**) and take a closer look at the <link> tag generated by the theme. It should resemble the one that follows:

```
<link href="../App_Themes/Sunny/Sunny.css"
      type="text/css" rel="stylesheet"/>
```

The URL stored in the <link> tag is a path that is relative to that of the template file. In this example, the preceding dot-dot-slash (../) characters indicate that the App_Themes folder is stored in the same parent folder as the current page. In a regular web application, referring to the style sheet using its relative path works correctly. After all, if you looked at the file structure, you can indeed find the style sheet at the suggested path.

However, when viewing a posting, we aren't accessing the template file directly. For example, to view the Aloe Vera posting, we request the URL http:// tropicalgreen/PlantCatalog/AloeVera.htm. The browser, not knowing that the MCMS ISAPI filter has rewritten the URL, attempts to retrieve the file by converting the relative path to the absolute path http://tropicalgreen/PlantCatalog/../App_Themes/Sunny/Sunny.css.

This path will, however, not evaluate to the real location of the CSS file, as the folder that's one-level above the AloeVera.htm page is tropicalgreen. Also, because the App_Themes folder is stored in the Templates project directory (see the following screenshot), looking for it under tropicalgreen (or the root website) will result in an HTTP 404 error.

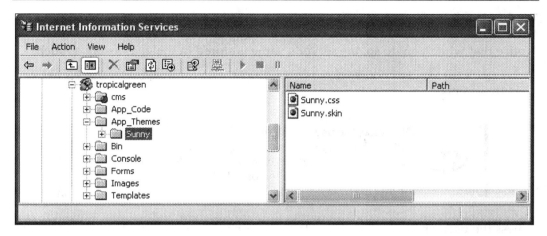

If using relative paths results in HTTP 404 errors when accessing the style sheet, how then, did the style get successfully applied to the posting? The secret lies in the `RobotMetaTag`. In MCMS websites, the `RobotMetaTag` has a `RenderBaseHref` property, which when set to `true` (its default value), will generate a `<base>` tag between the `<head>` tags of the page. Search the generated HTML source of the posting, and you will find the `<base>` tag that looks like the following:

```
<base href="http://tropicalgreen/tropicalgreen/Templates/Plant.aspx">
```

When evaluating links on a page, the web browser automatically prefixes all relative links with the value stored in the `href` attribute of the `<base>` tag (instead of the requesting URL for the page) such that a relative path like `../App_Themes/Sunny/Sunny.css` becomes `http://tropicalgreen/tropicalgreen/Templates/../App_Themes/Sunny/Sunny.css`.

The converted URL does lead to the style sheet, so we don't get any HTTP 404 errors.

By default, the `RenderBaseHref` property of the `RobotMetaTag` control stores the Boolean `true`. So usually, the `<base>` tag is generated and you won't have to worry about paths to style sheets and other relative links being inaccessible. However, depending on the site setup, there may be special situations where generating a `<base>` is not desirable.

Consider the case of a hosting scenario where a firewall or proxy forwards the request to an internal web server. The trouble with the MCMS-generated `<base>` tag is that it contains the full URL, which may include the server's name, especially when the "**map channels to host headers**" option has been turned off. When the internal server returns the page back to the proxy, the `<base>` tag of the returned page will contain the name of the *internal* server instead of the site's *domain name* as entered in the browser.

To simulate this scenario, try viewing the postings again, but this time by using a URL like `http://servername/tropicalgreen/plantcatalog/aloevera.htm`. Notice that when you do so, the server's name is stored in the `<base>` tag as such:

```
<base href="http://servername/tropicalgreen/tropicalgreen/Templates/
Plant.aspx ">
```

> Of course, the usual URL omits the server's name and will just be `http://tropicalgreen/plantcatalog/aloevera.htm`. But since we are testing to see how the server name creeps into the base URL, we have added it in for this exercise.

Unless the user's browser has access to the internal server, it will likely receive HTTP 404 errors when attempting to access resources like style sheets. In such cases, the `RenderBaseHref` property has to be disabled and an alternative solution found.

Applying Themes when the RenderBaseHref Property is Disabled

In case the `<base>` tag can't be used, we need to have a different way to ensure that the `App_Themes` folder is accessed with the correct URL. As ASP.NET has no way to configure the way it generates the URL to the theme's folder, we need to modify this URL after ASP.NET has generated it.

There are many ways to address the problem. We could manually add code to each and every template file that has the theme applied. However, not only would that be tedious, but repeating code in multiple places is also not good programming practice. We could create a server-side control to encapsulate the code and insert it into each template file that requires it. Again, this requires code for the control to be copied into every template file—there's still the possibility that it may get forgotten, especially when new templates are created.

The solution is to build an HTTP module. In this way, we can guarantee that all pages will have the correction without having to touch any of the existing template files. Before the page is sent to the browser, the HTTP module will convert all relative paths stored in `<link>` tags to absolute paths that do not contain the name of the server. The module will look for `<link>` tags such as the one for the style sheet:

```
<link href="../App_Themes/Sunny/Sunny.css" type="text/css"
rel="stylesheet"/>
```

After the conversion process, the `<link>` tag will be rendered as:

```
<link href="/tropicalgreen/App_Themes/Sunny/Sunny.css" type="text/css"
rel="stylesheet"/>
```

Creating the CorrectThemes HTTP Module

Let's create the HTTP module that corrects the URL stored in the `<link>` tags.

1. Add a new Visual C# Class Library project to the solution. Name the project **TropicalGreenHttpModules**.

2. Delete the `Class1.cs` file created by the wizard. We won't need it.

3. Add the following reference required by the project:

   `Microsoft.ContentManagement.Publishing.dll`

   (The library file is located in the `<install directory>\Microsoft Content Management Server\Server\bin\` directory).

   As well as the following references from the `System` namespace:

   `System.Web`

4. Add a class file to the **TropicalGreenHttpModules** project. Name the new class file **CorrectLinksInThemes.cs**.

5. Add the following `using` statements above the namespace declaration:

   ```
   using System;
   . . . code continues . . .

   using System.Web;
   using System.Web.UI;
   using System.Web.UI.HtmlControls;
   using Microsoft.ContentManagement.Publishing;

   namespace TropicalGreenHttpModules
   {
       . . . code continues . . .
   }
   ```

6. As we are creating an HTTP module, the class will implement the `IHttpModule` interface. Add a colon followed by the interface name as shown in the following code:

   ```
   public class CorrectLinksInThemes : IHttpModule
   {
   }
   ```

7. The `IHttpModule` requires the implementation of both the `Init()` and `Dispose()` methods. Add the following code to the `CorrectLinksInThemes` class file:

```
public class CorrectLinksInThemes : IHttpModule
{

    public void Init(HttpApplication httpApp)
    {
    }

    public void Dispose()
    {
    }
}
```

8. As all `<link>` tags stored in the page are analyzed before the page is rendered, we will write the code in the `OnPreRender()` event handler of the page object. The code loops through each control found in the page header. If the control is a `<link>` tag, it checks if the link is relative, and converts it to an absolute link if necessary. Add the `OnPreRender()` event handler below the `Dispose()` method.

```
public void OnPreRender(object sender, EventArgs eventArgs)
{
    Page currentPage = sender as Page;
    HtmlHead pageHeader = currentPage.Header as HtmlHead;
    if (pageHeader != null)
    {
        foreach (Control control in pageHeader.Controls)
        {
            HtmlLink link = control as HtmlLink;
            if (link != null &&
                VirtualPathUtility.IsAppRelative(link.Href))
            {
                link.Href = VirtualPathUtility.ToAbsolute
                                        (link.Href);
            }
        }
    }
}
```

9. We need to register the `OnPreRender()` event handler that we have written earlier to the `PreRender()` event of the page. A good place to do so would be within the `OnPreRequestHandlerExecute()` event handler of the current

HTTP application. The `OnPreRender()` event handler will only be registered if the request is for a `ChannelItem` (e.g. a channel-rendering script or a posting). We wrap the code around a `try-catch` block, as an exception may be raised if the page was requested when the user's form's login has expired. In such a case, we will ignore the error as the page will not be rendered.

```
public void OnPreRequestHandlerExecute(object sender, EventArgs e)
{
    HttpContext ctx = ((HttpApplication)sender).Context;
    IHttpHandler handler = ctx.Handler;

    // Only execute for ASP.NET page and master page
    // http handler - not for custom
    // http handler or for the ASP.NET 2.0 handler to handle
    // embedded resource items.
    // Check handler to see if it starts with "ASP."
    if (handler.GetType().ToString().StartsWith("ASP."))
    {
        try
        {
            if (CmsHttpContext.Current.ChannelItem != null)
            {
                ((System.Web.UI.Page)handler).PreRender +=
                          new EventHandler( this.OnPreRender);
            }
        }
        catch
        {
            // An exception may be raised if the request is made
            // in the middle of
            // an expired forms authentication login
            // Just ignore this.
        }
    }
}
```

10. Finally, we register the `OnPreRequestHandlerExecute()` event handler to the `PreRequestHanderExecute` event of the current `HttpApplication` within the `Init()` event of the HTTP module.

```
public void Init(HttpApplication httpApp)
{
```

```
httpApp.PreRequestHandlerExecute += new
    EventHandler(this.OnPreRequestHandlerExecute);
}
```

The HTTP module is complete. Save and build the project. To add the module to the **TropicalGreen** project, insert the following code in TropicalGreen's web.config file, between the <httpModules> tag.

```
<add type="TropicalGreenHttpModules.CorrectLinksInThemes,
        TropicalGreenHttpModules" name="CorrectLinksInThemes"/>
```

In addition, add the **TropicalGreenHttpModules** project (or the TropicalGreenHttpModules.dll library) as a reference to the **TropicalGreen** project.

The next time you view a posting with both themes applied and the RenderBaseHref property of the RobotMetaTag disabled, all style sheets will be correctly applied. Take a look at the HTML source, and you will find that the HTTP module has corrected all relative links to absolute links.

Summary

We have seen how themes can be used to efficiently manage the look and feel of an MCMS website. A theme consists of skins, cascading style sheets, and other supporting files. Together, skins and cascading style sheets effectively separate design elements from code.

While themes will work well on most MCMS websites, some sites may require some customization when the RenderBaseHref property of the RobotMetaTag has been disabled. This is because links to style sheets are rendered as relative links. As a workaround, a custom HTTP module could be built to correct the relative links on the page to absolute links.

6

Authentication Controls and Membership Providers

The Membership Provider Model is one of the new key concepts introduced with ASP.NET 2.0, which makes it significantly easier to develop web applications that utilize third-party or custom membership stores. In addition, ASP.NET 2.0 ships with a number of authentication controls related to role membership, which vastly reduce the amount of code required to implement Forms Authentication and associated functionality in your applications.

MCMS has its own role-based authorization and user management system that cannot be extended. However the Membership Provider Model and the shipped controls can be used within MCMS applications to improve the implementation of Forms Authentication and provide a more elegant solution for 'account mapping' scenarios whereby authentication takes place against an external store and the accounts are mapped to Windows accounts for the purposes of MCMS authorization.

In this chapter we will first briefly look at the ASP.NET 2.0 authentication controls, before proceeding to implement an MCMS Membership Provider that supports the use of the authentication controls within MCMS applications.

Authentication Controls

ASP.NET 2.0 ships with seven authentication-related composite controls such as the Login control (which provides a standard user interface for implementing Forms Authentication) and the PasswordRecovery control (which allows retrieval of a user's password). These controls can be seen within the **Login** tab of the Visual Studio 2005 toolbox.

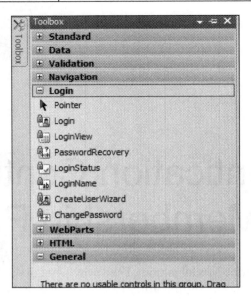

As MCMS has its own user management system that does not provide a supported API, only three of these controls can be used with MCMS applications:

- Login: provides the necessary user interface for Forms Authentication.

- LoginStatus: provides a **Login** or **Logout** hyperlink depending upon the user's current logon status.

- LoginName: displays the name of the currently logged-on user.

The LoginName control can be used directly without modification in MCMS applications regardless of their authentication mode to display the name of the currently logged-on user. The LoginStatus control, however, has no useful purpose unless Forms Authentication is being used where it can be used with a small amount of custom code to enable users to log in and out of MCMS applications.

The Login control can be used as an alternative to hand crafting the necessary code to implement forms-based authentication for MCMS applications. However, because of the MCMS authentication and authorization system, we must implement a Membership Provider that does the work behind the scenes to verify user credentials. By using this approach, it is also possible to manipulate the results from the MCMS authentication and authorization system such as adding extra detail to the returned user ticket.

Implementing an MCMS Membership Provider

In order to support MCMS applications, our MCMS Membership Provider has to implement the `ValidateUser()` method, which performs MCMS Forms Authentication. This is the method that will be called when a user submits his or her credentials from the `Login` control. The following example shows such an implementation:

```
public override bool ValidateUser(string strUsername,
                                  string strPassword)
{
    bool ValidUser = false;
    CmsAuthenticationTicket Ticket =
        CmsFormsAuthentication.AuthenticateAsUser(strUsername,
                                                  strPassword);

    if (Ticket != null)
    {
        ValidUser = true;
    }

    return ValidUser;
}
```

This code will generate an MCMS authentication ticket if authentication is successful. We could now directly call the `CmsFormsAuthentication.SetAuthCookie` to set the cookie, but the provider is not the right place to set the cookie. The `ValidateUser()` method should only verify if the user credentials provided are valid. In the provider, we would also not have access to the properties of the `Login` control, like the `RememberMeSet` checkbox, which gives the user the opportunity to decide whether the cookie should be persisted.

The correct place to set the authentication cookie is in the `LoggedIn` event of the `Login` control. The problem is that the Membership Provider Model doesn't allow us to pass the ticket back to the `Login` control. To overcome this limitation, we can add our MCMS ticket to the `Items` collection of the current `HttpContext`:

```
public override bool ValidateUser(string strUsername,
                                  string strPassword)
{
    bool ValidUser = false;
    CmsAuthenticationTicket Ticket =
        CmsFormsAuthentication.AuthenticateAsUser(strUsername,
                                                  strPassword);
```

```
        if (Ticket != null)
        {
            HttpContext.Current.Items.Add("MCMSTicket", Ticket);
            ValidUser = true;
        }


        return ValidUser;
    }
```

The `Items` collection is a bucket that can be used to pass all kind of objects between different code parts within one request—even between different `HttpModules`. The lifetime of the `HttpContext Items` collection is a single request. We can now utilize the MCMS ticket created by the Membership Provider within the `Login` control.

Now let's implement a Base Membership Provider class for MCMS. We will do this by creating a new Class Library Project rather than using the `App_Code` folder. Once complete, this can be reused across multiple MCMS applications.

By implementing a base Membership Provider, we can separate the code needed to interact with the MCMS authentication and authorization system from code used to manipulate credential format or interact with external authentication systems.

1. Open the **TropicalGreen** website in Visual Studio 2005.

2. Choose **Add** from the **File Menu**, followed by **New Project...**

3. In the **Add New project** dialog, select the **Class Library** icon in the **Visual Studio Installed Templates** section.

4. Enter **MCMSMembershipProviders** in the **Name** textbox, and click **OK**.

5. Delete the `Class1.cs` file.

6. Right-click **References** and click **Add Reference...**

7. In the **Add Reference** dialog, select the **System.Configuration** and **System.Web** components and click **OK**.

8. Right-click **References** and click **Add Reference...** In the **Add Reference** dialog, click the **Browse** tab.

9. Navigate to the `c:\Program Files\Microsoft Content Management Server\Server\bin` folder, select the `Microsoft.ContentManagement.Web.dll` file, and click **OK**.

10. Right-click the **MCMSMembershipProviders** project and click **Add**, followed by **New Item...**

11. In the **Add New Item** dialog, select the **Class** icon and enter **MCMSMembershipProviderBase** in the **Name** textbox. Click **OK**. Add the following `using` statements:

```
using System.Web;
using System.Web.Security;
using Microsoft.ContentManagement.Web.Security;
```

12. Modify the namespace declaration to:

```
TropicalGreen.MCMSMembershipProviders
```

13. Modify the class declaration to:

```
public abstract class MCMSMembershipProviderBase :
    System.Web.Security.MembershipProvider
```

14. Implement the following methods in the `MCMSMembershipProviderBase` class. (To avoid entering the following code, you can download it from the Packt website.)

```
public override bool ValidateUser(string strUsername,
                                  string strPassword)
{
    bool ValidUser = false;
    CmsAuthenticationTicket Ticket;

    Ticket = CmsFormsAuthentication.AuthenticateAsUser(strUsername,
                                                       strPassword);
    if (Ticket != null)
    {
    // pass the CmsAuthenticationTicket to the Login Control
    HttpContext.Current.Items.Add("MCMSTicket", Ticket);
    ValidUser = true;
    }
    return ValidUser;
}


public override bool EnablePasswordReset
{
    get { throw new Exception(
        "The method or operation is not implemented."); }
}
public override bool EnablePasswordRetrieval
{
    get { throw new Exception(
        "The method or operation is not implemented."); }
}
public override bool RequiresQuestionAndAnswer
{
    get { throw new Exception(
```

```
                          "The method or operation is not implemented."); }
        }
        public override string ApplicationName
        {
            get { throw new Exception(
                  "The method or operation is not implemented."); }
            set { throw new Exception(
                  "The method or operation is not implemented."); }
        }
        public override int MaxInvalidPasswordAttempts
        {
            get { throw new Exception(
                  "The method or operation is not implemented."); }
        }
        public override int PasswordAttemptWindow
        {
            get { throw new Exception(
                  "The method or operation is not implemented."); }
        }


        public override bool RequiresUniqueEmail
        {
            get { throw new Exception(
                  "The method or operation is not implemented."); }
        }
        public override MembershipPasswordFormat PasswordFormat
        {
            get { throw new Exception(
                  "The method or operation is not implemented."); }
        }
        public override int MinRequiredPasswordLength
        {
            get { throw new Exception(
                  "The method or operation is not implemented."); }
        }
        public override int MinRequiredNonAlphanumericCharacters
        {
            get { throw new Exception(
                  "The method or operation is not implemented."); }
        }
        public override string PasswordStrengthRegularExpression
        {
            get { throw new Exception(
                  "The method or operation is not implemented."); }
```

```
}
public override MembershipUser CreateUser(string username,
                    string password, string email,
                    string passwordQuestion, string passwordAnswer,
                    bool isApproved, object providerUserKey,
                    out MembershipCreateStatus status)
{
    throw new Exception(
        "The method or operation is not implemented.");
}
public override bool ChangePassword(string username,
                            string oldPassword, string
                            newPassword)
{
    throw new Exception(
        "The method or operation is not implemented.");
}
public override string GetPassword(string username, string answer)
{
    throw new Exception(
        "The method or operation is not implemented.");
}
public override string ResetPassword(string username, string answer)
{
    throw new Exception(
        "The method or operation is not implemented.");
}
public override void UpdateUser(MembershipUser user)
{
    throw new Exception(
        "The method or operation is not implemented.");
}
public override MembershipUserCollection GetAllUsers(int pageIndex,
                            int pageSize, out int totalRecords)
{
    throw new Exception(
        "The method or operation is not implemented.");
}
public override bool ChangePasswordQuestionAndAnswer(string username,
                    string password, string newPasswordQuestion,
                    string newPasswordAnswer)
{
    throw new Exception(
        "The method or operation is not implemented.");
```

```
     }
     public override bool UnlockUser(string userName)
     {
          throw new Exception(
               "The method or operation is not implemented.");
     }
     public override MembershipUser GetUser(object providerUserKey,
                                            bool userIsOnline)
     {
          throw new Exception(
               "The method or operation is not implemented.");
     }
     public override MembershipUser GetUser(string username,
                                            bool userIsOnline)
     {
          throw new Exception(
               "The method or operation is not implemented.");
     }
     public override string GetUserNameByEmail(string email)
     {
          throw new Exception(
               "The method or operation is not implemented.");
     }
     public override bool DeleteUser(string username,
                                     bool deleteAllRelatedData)
     {
          throw new Exception(
               "The method or operation is not implemented.");
     }
     public override int GetNumberOfUsersOnline()
     {
          throw new Exception(
               "The method or operation is not implemented.");
     }
     public override MembershipUserCollection FindUsersByName(
                                string usernameToMatch,
                                int pageIndex,
                                int pageSize, out int totalRecords)
     {
          throw new Exception(
               "The method or operation is not implemented.");
     }
     public override MembershipUserCollection FindUsersByEmail(
                                string emailToMatch,
```

```
                                          int pageIndex,
                                          int pageSize,
                                          out int totalRecords)
    {
        throw new Exception(
            "The method or operation is not implemented.");

    }
```

 Notice that many methods simply throw an exception when called. These methods are related to functionality (for example, "password reset") only relevant to a custom authentication schema that supports such functionality.

15. Save and build the **MCMSMembershipProviders** project.

Now let's implement a simple MCMS Membership Provider for Windows accounts based on our abstract class that simply formats the user name correctly before calling the `ValidateUser()` method in the base class.

1. Right-click the **MCMSMembershipProviders** project and click **Add**, followed by **New Item...** In the **Add New Item** dialog, select the **Class** icon and enter **MCMSWindowsMembershipProvider** in the **Name** textbox. Click **OK**.

2. Modify the namespace declaration to:
```
TropicalGreen.MCMSMembershipProviders
```

3. Modify the class declaration to:
```
public class McmsWindowsMembershipProvider :
MCMSMembershipProviderBase
```

4. Implement the following in the `McmsWindowsMembershipProvider` class:
```
public override bool ValidateUser
    (string strName, string strPassword)
{
    string strLogin = "WinNT://" + strName.Replace("\\", "/");
    return base.ValidateUser(strLogin, strPassword);
}
```

For brevity, the sample code here does not include any input validation or exception handling, and assumes that the format of `strName` is `MachineOrDomainName\username`. For production applications, we would implement exception handling and input validation.

5. Save and build the **MCMSMembershipProviders** project.

Using an MCMS Membership Provider

Now that we have created our MCMS Membership Provider, we need to register it with our Tropical Green MCMS application.

1. Right-click the **TropicalGreen** website and click **Add Reference...**

2. In the **Add Reference** dialog, click the **Projects** tab.

3. Click **MCMSMembershipProviders** and **OK**.

4. Open the `web.config` file.

5. Add the following section directly below the existing `<authentication />` tag:

```
<membership defaultProvider="McmsWindowsMembershipProvider"
                            userIsOnlineTimeWindow="30">
  <providers>
    <add name="McmsWindowsMembershipProvider"
         type="TropicalGreen.MCMSMembershipProviders.
         McmsWindowsMembershipProvider"
         applicationName="/"/>
  </providers>
</membership>
```

Note that the `type` attribute of the `<add>` element needs to be entered on one line with no spaces or line breaks. The formatting above is for printing purposes only.

6. Modify the authentication section to use Forms Authentication:

```
<authentication mode="Forms">
  <forms loginUrl="Login.aspx"/>
</authentication>
```

Creating a Login Page Using the Login Control

Now let's go ahead and implement a login page allowing users to sign in, which will utilize the new ASP.NET 2.0 login controls.

1. Right-click the **TropicalGreen** website, and click **Add New Item.**

2. Select the **Web Form** icon, enter **Login.aspx** in the **Name** textbox and click **Add**. Ensure that the **Select Master Page** checkbox is not selected.

> Adding a Login control to a master page will work. However if the master page includes code that interacts with the PAPI (such as navigation controls or posting properties), your MCMS installation will require Guest access to be enabled. Such an implementation is only appropriate for mixed authoring and read-only hosting scenarios that utilize Forms Authentication.

3. Switch to **Design** view.

4. From the toolbox **Login** tab, drag a **Login** control onto the design surface.

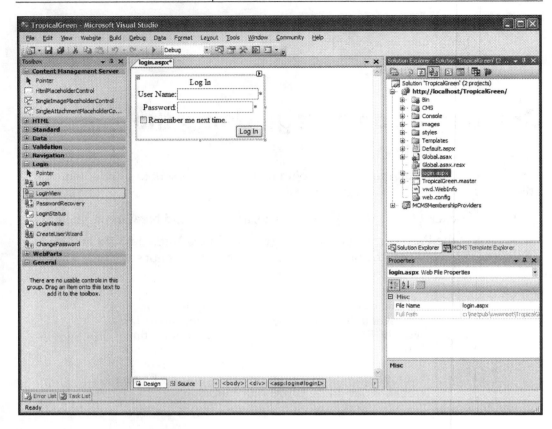

5. If desired, use the Login control's **Auto Format** task to select a format scheme.

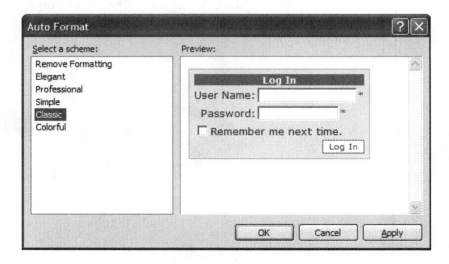

6. Click the `Login` control (**Login1**) and then the events icon (the lightning bolt) in the **Property** window.

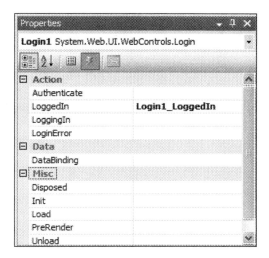

7. Double-click the **LoggedIn** event to add the `Login1_LoggedIn` event handler and jump to it in **Code** view.

8. Add the following `using` statement:

```
using Microsoft.ContentManagement.Web.Security;
```

9. Implement the following directly beneath the `Page_Load` method:

```
protected void Login1_LoggedIn(object sender, EventArgs e)
{
        Login myLogin = sender as Login;

        if (HttpContext.Current.Items.Contains("MCMSTicket"))
        {
                CmsAuthenticationTicket Ticket =
                        HttpContext.Current.Items["MCMSTicket"]
                        as CmsAuthenticationTicket;
                CmsFormsAuthentication.SetAuthCookie(Ticket,
                                false, Login1.RememberMeSet);
        }
}
```

10. From the **Build** menu, choose **Build Web Site**.

Now that we have completed our login page, we can go ahead and test the functionality in Internet Explorer by browsing to `http://localhost/tropicalgreen`.

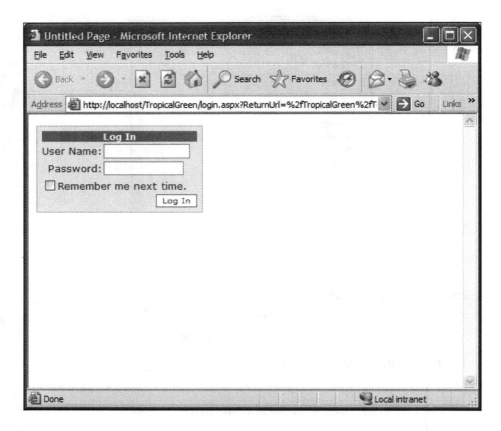

11. Enter your user name and password and click **Log In**. Remember to enter your user name in the format **MachineOrDomainName\username**.

12. If your credentials are correct, you will be logged in and taken to the Tropical Green home page. Otherwise a message will be displayed in the `Login` control.

Using the LoginStatus and LoginName Controls

Now we have a login page we can use the `LoginStatus` and `LoginName` controls to provide the additional membership-related functionality in our templates. Let's go ahead and add these controls to our master page.

1. Open `TropicalGreen.master` in **Design** view.

2. From the **Login** tab of the toolbox, drag a **LoginStatus** control to the right-hand table cell above the existing menu control (**MenuRight**).

3. Click the `LoginStatus` control (**LoginStatus1**) and the events icon in the **Property** window.

4. Double-click the **LoggedOut** event to add the `Login1_LoggedOut` event handler and jump to it in **Code** view.

5. Add the following `using` statement:

   ```
   using Microsoft.ContentManagement.Web.Security;
   ```

6. Implement the following directly beneath the `Page_Load` method:

   ```
   protected void LoginStatus1_LoggedOut(object sender, EventArgs e)
   {
       CmsFormsAuthentication.SignOut();
   }
   ```

7. Save your work, and from the **Build** menu, choose **Build Web Site**.

We can now test the `LoginStatus` control by logging in to our site:

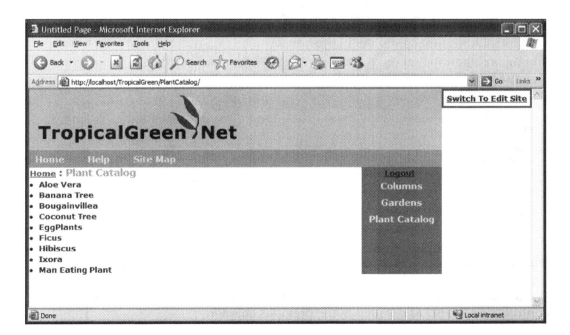

When we click the **Logout** link, we are signed out of MCMS and returned to our login page. If Guest access was enabled on our MCMS installation, the LoginStatus control would display a **Login** link.

Let's now go ahead and add a LoginName control to our master page:

1. Open TropicalGreen.master in **Design** view.

2. From the **Login** tab of the toolbox, drag a **LoginName** control to the right-hand table cell above the existing LoginStatus control.

3. Switch to **Source** view.

4. After the <asp:LoginName /> element, add a non-breaking space:

   ```
   <asp:LoginName ID="LoginName1" runat="server"/>
   <br/>
   ```

5. Save your work and from the **Build** menu choose **Build Web Site**.

Now when we are logged in, we can see the name of the currently logged-in user:

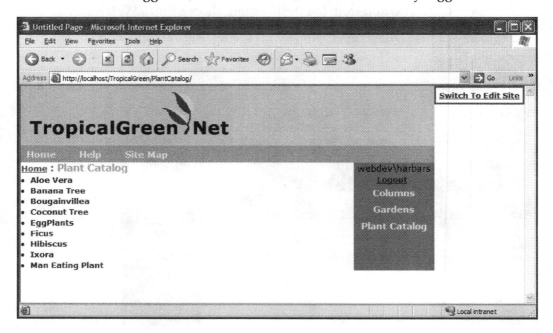

We could easily enhance the look and feel of the LoginStatus and LoginName controls using skins as detailed in the previous chapter.

Supporting Custom Authentication Schemes

So far we've seen how to make use of the new ASP.NET 2.0 login controls by creating an MCMS Membership Provider for Windows accounts and using it with Forms Authentication. It is also possible to use the same approach to provide a more elegant solution for "account mapping" scenarios whereby authentication takes place against an external user store.

For example, suppose we needed to use Active Directory Application Mode (ADAM) for authentication, we could implement an ADAM Membership Provider based upon our MCMSMembershipProviderBase class by overriding the ValidateUser() method:

```
using System.DirectoryServices;
... Code Continues . . .
public override bool ValidateUser(string strName, string strPassword)
{
    // the LDAP server to connect to
    string strLdapServer = "LDAP://localhost:389/";
    // the DN of the OU containing the user
    string strLdapObj = "OU=MCMSUsers,O=TropicalGreen";
    // the DirectoryEntry property to validate
    string strDECheck = "MCMSUsers";
    // the DN of the user we are connecting as
    string strBindName = "CN=" + strName + "," + strLdapObj;
    // the Windows Username format for pasing to ValidateUser
    string strWindowsUser = "WinNT://webdev/" + strName;

    try
    {
        // Connect to ADAM using LDAP AuthN...
        DirectoryEntry ent = new DirectoryEntry(strLdapServer +
                strLdapObj, strBindName,
                strPassword, AuthenticationTypes.None);

        // We must bind to perform authentication
        if ((string)ent.Properties["name"].Value == strDECheck)
        {
            // LDAP AuthN succeeded, so perform Windows
            // AuthN to setup a MCMS context...
            return base.ValidateUser(strWindowsUser, strPassword);
        }
        // LDAP AuthN failed, so return a false
```

```
        return false;
    }

catch (Exception)
    {
        //LDAP AuthN failed, so return a false
        return false;
    }
}
```

 Active Directory Application Mode (ADAM) is a standalone LDAP 3 directory service. The above sample assumes that ADAM is installed on the same machine as MCMS, is configured to allow unsecured operation, MCMS users are stored within an Organizational Unit named **MCMSUsers**, and that passwords are identical in both ADAM and Active Directory or the Local Security Accounts (SAM) database.

The above sample could be extended to create Windows and ADAM user accounts and provide additional functionality, such as password reset, to end users. However, there remains no supported mechanism to manage MCMS Role Group membership. An appropriate compromise is to create a Windows group for each MCMS Role Group. The Windows group is then added to the MCMS Role Group using **Site Manager**, and users can be added to the Windows group programmatically.

Summary

We have covered using the new ASP.NET 2.0 Login controls and Membership Provider Model by creating an MCMS Membership Provider for Windows Accounts and using it with Forms Authentication. We also learned which controls are useful to MCMS applications and how to integrate them with our MCMS applications. We have also seen how to make use of these ASP.NET 2.0 features to enhance "account mapping" scenarios by developing a Membership Provider for an external authentication system.

7

How-Tos, Tips, and Tricks

ASP.NET 2.0 introduces many exciting new tools. In this chapter, we have put together several tips that you can use to enhance your sites:

- **Tip #1: How to Perform Cross-Page Postbacks**: ASP.NET 2.0 introduces a new way of passing data from page to page. Instead of having all forms post data back to themselves, you may now specify an alternative form to post the data to. In this tip, we will take a look at how cross-page postbacks can be done, and the workaround required for it to be successfully implemented on MCMS pages.

- **Tip #2: How to Implement an Ad Rotator**: While the Ad Rotator existed in earlier versions of ASP and ASP.NET, the latest version that ships with ASP. NET 2.0 has the ability to programmatically access the data source. In this tip, we will build a server control that shows how you can integrate the Ad Rotator control directly with an MCMS resource gallery.

- **Tip #3: Considerations for Microsoft Office SharePoint Server 2007**: In preparation for the upcoming release of Office SharePoint Portal Server, we take a look at some of the things that should be considered to make the migration of code easier.

Tip #1: How to Perform Cross-Page Postbacks

Previously in ASP.NET 1.x, web forms were designed to submit information (or post back) only to themselves. Doing so offered the convenience of performing server-side processing within the page itself. Events like button clicks, page loads, and form submissions could be handled from the page's code-behind file. However, because the form could only post to itself, sharing data across pages became a tricky and messy affair.

ASP.NET 2.0 introduces the `PostBackUrl` property to the `Button`, `LinkButton`, and `ImageButton` controls. With the `PostBackUrl` property, developers may now send postback data to any web form within the site. This feature is particularly useful when working with multiple web forms that share data or interact with one another.

In this tip, we will take a look at the `PostBackUrl` feature as well as an essential workaround required for it to work correctly on MCMS sites. Here's what we will be building. We will start by creating a page that accepts input from a user. Next, we will add a button that has its `PostBackUrl` property set to another page. Following which, we will build the page specified in the `PostBackUrl` property of the button and program it to accept the inputs from the first page. Finally, we will take a look at some required workarounds for `PostBackUrl` properties to work correctly in MCMS sites.

Passing Data between Pages

A common scenario where data is passed from page to page is to have a search input field on all your postings or a dedicated search page that contains fields for entering keywords and other criteria. The entered search criteria could be submitted to a separate page that performs the search and displays the results.

Or you may have a ubiquitous wizard-style dialog similar to the ones found in popular online stores like Amazon or eBay. Wizards break down a task (say, checking out the items in a shopping basket) into a series of individual steps. Information such as the list of items in the shopping basket, the user's name, shipping address, and other details are passed from page to page until the transaction is finally committed.

One way of tackling the problem would be to place all sections of the wizard in a single web form. The sections are usually managed by panels or tables. As the user progresses through the task, he or she sees only a portion of the page. Sections not related to the step he or she is working on are hidden from view. In this way, the user never leaves the page. However, the main drawback to this approach is that as the sections increase in both number and complexity, the page becomes progressively more difficult to maintain.

Alternatively, you could call `Server.Transfer()`, which accepts an input parameter that indicates whether the state and values input fields should be preserved when directing from one page to another. For example, in `Page1.aspx`, we could call `Page2.aspx` as follows:

```
Server.Transfer("Page2.aspx", true);
```

By setting the second, Boolean parameter to `true`, the state of all form values will be passed to `Page2.aspx`. From `Page2.aspx`, we can retrieve input field values using the `Request.Form` collection:

```
string myText = Request.Form["MyText"];
```

However, `Server.Transfer()` suffers from several drawbacks. Firstly, the URL on the address bar remains the same from page to page, which may not be desirable. More importantly, `Server.Transfer()` cannot be used in combination with MCMS pages because it bypasses the ISAPI filter.

Another solution would be to pass the entire chunk of information using query strings. Nevertheless, query strings suffer from a couple of limitations. Not only do long query strings create unfriendly looking URLs, the value is exposed in the address bar of the browser, giving users the opportunity to alter its value causing the application to behave unexpectedly. Also, if the length exceeds the maximum allowable length of a query string, data may get lost along the way.

You could even store the data in session variables or in database tables. While these methods work, they are expensive to implement and may result in performance issues. For example, session objects are usually stored in the server's memory. Maintaining the session state of thousands of simultaneous users may take up a significant amount of memory—and if not managed properly may cause a site to crash.

With so many pitfalls and considerations, how then should we pass data from one page to another? The new `PostBackUrl` property in button controls offers an attractive alternative. Instead of managing the page's state in sections or intermediate storage locations like query strings, session objects, or database tables, we can simply post the data directly to another form. Let's take a look at how it's implemented.

The "Order a Plant" Wizard

To demonstrate how the `PostBackUrl` property works, we will create a wizard that guides visitors through the process of ordering plants from the TropicalGreen society. To keep things simple, we will just have two screens.

In the first screen, visitors will enter their name and address. They will also select a plant from a drop-down list.

First Name:	
Last Name:	
Address:	
Select a Plant	Aloe Vera
	Order

The second screen will print the values entered by the visitor in the first screen and provides a button to confirm the order.

The Ordering Page

Let's start by creating the order page.

1. To begin, add a folder named `Forms` to the TropicalGreen solution.

2. Add a web form to the `Forms` folder. Name the form `Order.aspx` and apply the `tropicalgreen.master` master page created earlier.

3. Toggle to **Source** view. Add the following code between `<asp:Content>` tags. The table holds the layout of the controls that we will be adding later.

```
<h1>Order a Plant</h1>
<table>
    <tr>
        <td>
            First Name:
        </td>
        <td>(TextBox for the First Name)</td>
    </tr>
    <tr>
        <td>
            Last Name:
        </td>
        <td>(TextBox for the Last Name)</td>
    </tr>

    <tr>
        <td>
            Shipping Address:
        </td>
    <td>(TextBox for the Shipping Address)</td>
    </tr>
    <tr>
```

```
      <td>Select a Plant</td>
      <td>(Dropdown list for the selection of plants)</td>
   </tr>
   <tr>
      <td colspan="2" align="right">
         (Button to Check Out)
      </td>
   </tr>
</table>
```

4. We will have fields for the customer to enter his or her first name, last name, and the shipping address, as well as the plant he or she would like to order. Switch back to **Design** view. Drag three **TextBoxes**, a **DropdownList**, and a **Button** control from the **Standard** section of the toolbox and place them as shown in the following screenshot:

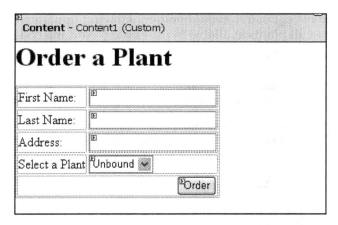

Give the controls the following property values:

Control	Property	Property Value
TextBox	ID	txtFirstName
TextBox	ID	txtLastName
TextBox	ID	txtAddress
DropDownList	ID	ddlPlant
Button	ID	btnOrder
	Text	Order
	PostBackUrl	/tropicalgreen/forms/checkout.aspx

Notice that we have set the PostBackUrl property of the button to point to a page named checkout.aspx (which we will be building in the next section). Instead of having the results post back to the current page, the data will be sent to checkout.aspx.

5. Double-click anywhere on the form to get to the code-behind file. At the top of the page, add the highlighted namespace.

```
using System;
. . . code continues . . .
using Microsoft.ContentManagement.Publishing;

public partial class Forms_Order : System.Web.UI.Page
{
    . . . code continues . . .
}
```

6. Within the Page_Load() event handler, we will populate the drop-down list with a list of all plants available in the catalog. Add the code as shown here:

```
protected void Page_Load(object sender, EventArgs e)
{
    // Get the current context
    CmsHttpContext cmsContext = CmsHttpContext.Current;

    // Get an instance of the plant catalog
    Channel plantCatalog = cmsContext.Searches.GetByPath(
            "/Channels/tropicalgreen/PlantCatalog") as Channel;

    if (plantCatalog != null)
    {
        // Get a collection of all postings in the plant catalog
        // channel
        PostingCollection plants = plantCatalog.Postings;

        // Sort the postings by display name
        plants.SortByDisplayName();

        // Populate the dropdown with a list of plants from the
        // catalog
        foreach (Posting plant in plants)
        {
         ListItem li =
                new ListItem(plant.DisplayName, plant DisplayName);
         ddlPlant.Items.Add(li);
        }
    }
}
```

7. To make it easier to retrieve the field values later on in the checkout process, we will create properties that return the text entered in the `txtFirstName`, `txtLastName`, and `txtAddress` textboxes. We will also add a property that returns the name of the selected plant from the drop-down list. Append the following code directly below the `Page_Load()` event handler.

```csharp
// First Name
public string FirstName
{
    get
    {
        return txtFirstName.Text.Trim();
    }
}

// Last Name
public string LastName
{
    get
    {
        return txtLastName.Text.Trim();
    }
}

// Address
public string Address
{
    get
    {
        return txtAddress.Text.Trim();
    }
}

// Plant
public string Plant
{
    get
    {
        return ddlPlant.SelectedItem.Value.Trim();
    }
}
```

The Checkout Screen

The checkout page will receive the values entered in the ordering screen and display them on the screen. When a user is satisfied that the information is correct, he or she clicks on the **Checkout** button, and a message appears informing her or him that the order has been successfully placed.

1. Add a web form to the `Forms` folder. Name the form `checkout.aspx` and set `tropicalgreen.master` to be the master page.

2. In **Source** view, add the following code between the `<asp:Content>` tags:

```
<h1>Checkout</h1>
<table>
    <tr>
        <td>First Name:</td>
        <td>(Space for First Name Label)</td>
    </tr>
    <tr>
        <td>Last Name:</td>
        <td>(Space for Last Name Label)</td>
    </tr>

    <tr>
        <td>Address:</td>
        <td>(Space for Address Label)</td>
    </tr>
    <tr>
        <td>Plant:</td>
        <td>(Space for Plant Label)</td>
    </tr>
    <tr>
        <td colspan="2" align="right">
            (Space for Confirm Button)
        </td>
    </tr>
</table>
(Space for Message Label)
```

3. Toggle to **Design** view. Drag and drop five Label controls and a **Button** control onto the form, arranging them as shown in the following screenshot:

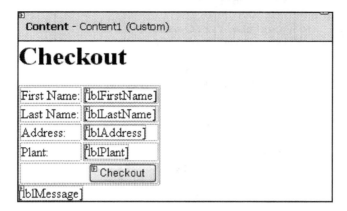

Assign the following property values to the controls:

Control	Property	Property Value
Label	ID	lblFirstName
Label	ID	lblLastName
Label	ID	lblAddress
Label	ID	lblPlant
Button	ID	btnCheckOut
	Text	Checkout
Label	ID	lblMessage

4. Earlier, when building the order form, we created a few properties that returned the values entered by the user. For the checkout page to retrieve these values easily, we will first strongly type the order page using the `PreviousPageType` directive. Switch to **Source** view and add the following line of code at the top of the page, below the `<%@Page%>` directive.

```
<%@ PreviousPageType VirtualPath="~/Forms/Order.aspx"%>
```

5. Switch to **Design** view and double-click anywhere on the form to get to its `Page_Load()` event handler in the code-behind file. Here, we will retrieve the data posted from the ordering page and assign them to the labels. To do so, we will retrieve the values stored in the `FirstName`, `LastName`, `Address`, and `Plant` properties created earlier.

```
protected void Page_Load(object sender, EventArgs e)
{
    if (!Page.IsPostBack)
    {
        // Get the first name
        lblFirstName.Text = PreviousPage.FirstName;

        // Get the last name
        lblLastName.Text = PreviousPage.LastName;

        // Get the address
        lblAddress.Text = PreviousPage.Address;

        // Get the plant
        lblPlant.Text = PreviousPage.Plant;
    }
}
```

6. Toggle back to **Design** view and double-click on the btnConfirm button to get to the btnConfirm_Click() event handler. Here, we will simply notify the user that the order has been successfully placed. Of course, in an actual website, you would probably do more than just print a message on the screen.

```
protected void btnConfirm_Click(object sender, EventArgs e)
{
    lblMessage.Text = "Plant has been successfully ordered.";
}
```

7. The page is complete. Save and build the website.

Adding the "Order Plants" Menu Item

Now that we have created both the ordering and order confirmation screens, let's add a new item to the right menu for our "Order a Plant" wizard to give visitors to the site access to it. Recall that the menus are driven by the site's channel structure. Therefore to add a menu item, we will simply insert a new channel and set its script URL to point to the order page.

1. Open **Site Manager** and log in with an account that has administrator privileges.

2. Create a channel directly under the **tropicalgreen** channel. Give the new channel the following property values:

Property	Property Value
Name	OrderPlant
DisplayName	Order Plants
Script URL	/tropicalgreen/forms/order.aspx

3. Once the channel has been created, create a selection type custom property named **MenuLocation** and assign it the following options:

   ° Top

   ° Right (make it the default value)

The "Order a Plant" menu item should now appear on the left menu.

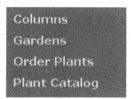

Why Cross-Page Postbacks Do Not Work on MCMS Sites

Navigate to any page within the website and click **Order a Plant**. In the ordering page, enter your first name, last name, and address, select a plant, and click on the **Order** button.

The page will refresh. The page seems to be posting back to itself even though we have set the PostBackUrl property of the button to a different page!

To understand why cross-page postbacks do not work on MCMS pages, let's take a look at the client script of the generated page. Observe the code generated for the btnOrder button (right-click anywhere on the page and select **View Source**), which resembles the following code:

```
<input type="submit"
name="ctl00$ContentPlaceHolder1$btnOrder"
value="Order"
onclick="javascript:
```

```
WebForm_DoPostBackWithOptions(new
WebForm_PostBackOptions(&quot;ctl00$ContentPlaceHolder1$btnOrder&quo
t;, &quot;&quot;, false, &quot;&quot;, &quot;/tropicalgreen/Forms/
CheckOut.aspx&quot;, false, false))" id="ctl00_ContentPlaceHolder1_
btnOrder"/>
```

Notice that the `onclick()` event handler calls a JavaScript method, `WebForm_DoPostBackWithOptions()`. This method is generated by ASP.NET whenever a button's `UrlPostBack` property has been set. The code that follows shows a snippet of what's happening behind the scenes. Note that the `action` attribute of the `form` element is set to that of the value stored in the `PostBackUrl` property of the button before submitting the form. Essentially, that's how the cross-postback function works.

```
function WebForm_DoPostBackWithOptions(options)
{
    . . . code continues . . .

    if ((typeof(options.actionUrl) != "undefined") &&
        (options.actionUrl != null) &&
        (options.actionUrl.length > 0))
    {
        theForm.action = options.actionUrl;
    }
    . . . code continues . . .

}
```

Scroll a little further down to the bottom of the page. Notice that before the closing `</form>` tag, MCMS has generated its own set of client-side scripts. In particular, take a look at the method named `__cmsRestFormAction()` (shown below). The `__cmsRestFormAction()` method sets the `action` attribute of the `form` element to the URL of the current page when the Boolean variable `__CMS_PostbackFormBeenReset` is set to `false`, thereby overriding any work done by the `WebForm_DoPostBackWithOptions()` method. Hence, when the button is clicked, instead of posting the information to the checkout page, the orders page continues to post back to itself.

```
var __CMS_PostbackFormBeenReset = false;
function __cmsRestFormAction()
{
    if ( !__CMS_PostbackFormBeenReset )
    {
        // set form postback Url to be current translated CMS Url
        __CMS_PostbackForm.action = __CMS_CurrentUrl;
    }
}
```

To correct this problem, we need modify the behavior of the client-side scripts added by MCMS to set `__CMS_PostbackFormBeenReset` to `true` when performing cross-page postbacks. Here's how it may be done.

- First, we will identify whether cross-page postbacks are required. To do so, we look for a method named `WebForm_DoPostBackWithOptions()`. The `WebForm_DoPostBackWithOptions()` method is an enhancement of the old ASP.NET 1.x `__doPostBack()` method and is injected by ASP.NET whenever at least one button on the page performs a cross postback.

- Next, we make a copy of the original `WebForm_DoPostBackWithOptions()` method and store it in a variable named `__CrossPostBack_Backup_WebForm_DoPostBackWithOptions`.

- Following this, we assign `WebForm_DoPostBackWithOptions()` a new method named `__CrossPostBack_Redirect_WebForm_DoPostBackWithOptions()`.

- The `__CrossPostBack_Redirect_WebForm_DoPostBackWithOptions()` method simply sets `__CMS_PostbackFormBeenReset` to `true` and calls the original `WebForm_DoPostBackWithOptions()` method, which we have backed up in the `__CrossPostBack_Backup_WebForm_DoPostBackWithOptions` variable.

Don't worry about typing the code for now. We will be injecting the code on all pages using server-side code in the next section.

```
if ( typeof WebForm_DoPostBackWithOptions != "undefined" )
{
    __CrossPostBack_Backup_WebForm_DoPostBackWithOptions =
                                WebForm_DoPostBackWithOptions;

    WebForm_DoPostBackWithOptions =
            __CrossPostBack_Redirect_WebForm_DoPostBackWithOptions;
}

function __CrossPostBack_Redirect_WebForm_DoPostBackWithOptions(options)
{
    __CMS_PostbackFormBeenReset = true;
    __CrossPostBack_Backup_WebForm_DoPostBackWithOptions(options);
}
```

The CorrectCrossPostBack HTTP Module

As the modification to the client-side script possibly influences all template files in the solution, a good way to implement the change would be to write an HTTP module. HTTP modules intercept all page requests, and can be programmed to automatically inject the modified scripts to all template files that require them.

To create the HTTP module, start by checking if the `TropicalGreenHttpModules` class library exists in the solution. If it doesn't, add it as a new Visual C# Class Library.

Next, add a class named `CorrectCrossPostBack.cs` to the `TropicalGreenHttpModules` class library. Above the class declaration, add the namespaces highlighted here:

```
. . . code continues . . .

using System.Web;
using Microsoft.ContentManagement.Publishing;

namespace TropicalGreenHttpModules
{
    . . . code continues . . .
}
```

Since we are building an HTTP module, let's have the class implement the `IHttpModule` interface.

```
class CorrectCrossPostBack : IHttpModule
{
}
```

The `IHttpModule` interface requires the class to implement the `Init()` and `Dispose()` methods. We won't need to do anything within the `Dispose()` method.

In the `Init()` method, we will register a new event handler named `OnPreRequestHandlerExecute()` to the `PreRequestHanderExecute` event of the HTTP module. Append both methods to the class file.

```
public void Dispose()
{
    // Nothing to do.
}


public void Init(HttpApplication httpApp)
{
```

```
httpApp.PreRequestHandlerExecute += new EventHandler
                              (this.OnPreRequestHandlerExecute);
}
```

Next, we will add the `OnPreRequestHandlerExecute()` event handler, which checks if the current request is that for an ASP (or ASP.NET) page. To do so, it checks if the handler's type begins with `ASP`. The HTTP module will ignore all other requests, such as those for ASP.NET 2.0 resource handlers or other custom handlers.

Within the `OnPreRequestHandlerExecute()` event handler, we will make another check to see if the request is for an MCMS channel item. If it is, we will register yet another event handler, `OnInit()`.

```
public void OnPreRequestHandlerExecute(object sender, EventArgs e)
{
    HttpContext ctx = ((HttpApplication)sender).Context;
    IHttpHandler handler = ctx.Handler;

    // Only execute for ASP.NET handler
    // not for custom http handlers or for the ASP.NET 2.0 resource
    // handlers.
    if (handler.GetType().ToString().StartsWith("ASP."))
    {
        try
        {
            if (CmsHttpContext.Current.ChannelItem != null)
            {
                ((System.Web.UI.Page)handler).Init += new
                    EventHandler(this.OnInit);
            }
        }
        catch
        {
            // This will happen if the request is in the middle of an
            // expired forms authentication login we just ignore this.
        }
    }
}
```

Finally, we will inject the client-side scripts that correct the problem with cross-page postbacks. We will build the script and use the `Page.ClientScript.RegisterStartUpScript()` method within the `OnInit()` method.

```
string Override_WebForm_DoPostBackWithOptions =
    "    if ( typeof WebForm_DoPostBackWithOptions != \"undefined\" )\n" +
```

```
"     {\n" +
"         __CrossPostBack_Backup_WebForm_DoPostBackWithOptions = " +
"                  WebForm_DoPostBackWithOptions;\n" +
"         WebForm_DoPostBackWithOptions = " +
"                  __CrossPostBack_Redirect_WebForm_
                  DoPostBackWithOptions;\n" +
"     }\n" +
"     function __CrossPostBack_Redirect_WebForm_DoPostBackWithOption
     s(options)" +
"     {\n" +
"         __CMS_PostbackFormBeenReset = true;\n" +
"         __CrossPostBack_Backup_WebForm_DoPostBackWithOptions
         (options);\n" +
"     }\n";

public void OnInit(object sender, EventArgs eventArgs)
{
    System.Web.UI.Page currentPage = sender as System.Web.UI.Page;
    currentPage.ClientScript.RegisterStartupScript(this.GetType(),
            "Override_WebForm_DoPostBackWithOptions",
            Override_WebForm_DoPostBackWithOptions, true);
}
```

The class is complete. Save and build the project.

To use the HTTP module, add the following entry to the `<HttpModules>` section of the `web.config` project.

```
<add type="TropicalGreenHttpModules.CorrectCrossPostBack,
TropicalGreenHttpModules"
    name="CorrectCrossPostBack"/>
```

Now, let's see if the HTTP module has indeed corrected the problem. Attempt to order a plant from the ordering page. When the **Order** button is clicked, notice that the information gets posted correctly to the confirmation page.

Tip #2: How to Implement an Ad Rotator

Advertisements are everywhere these days. On most commercial Internet websites, you will find some form of advertising either as banners running along the height or width of the page or as pop-up windows grabbing attention whenever a page loads.

Popular sites will probably have multiple advertisers requesting to put up their advertisements online. When the competition gets hot, a process must be devised to determine whose ads appear first, how the ads should be ordered, and when they should be published or taken offline.

The good news is: ASP.NET 2.0 ships with an Ad Rotator control. In this tip, we will take a look at how the Ad Rotator can be integrated with MCMS resource-gallery items. Using the MCMS built-in Resource Manager, users may add new images or replace existing ones without worrying about broken hyperlinks. And when an image is deleted from the gallery, it is immediately taken offline.

While the Ad Rotator isn't a new control and has been around since the ASP.NET 1.x days (and even before that), older versions of the control required developers to define the list of advertisements in a physical XML file. The enhanced version of the control allows for programmatic population of the ads as well as their properties and makes it perfect for integrating with MCMS.

The MCMSAdRotator

Let's build a custom Ad Rotator server control. When completed, the control behaves exactly like the out-of-the box Ad Rotator control, but integrates with a selected resource gallery. It will pick a resource at random from the gallery and display the image. When the page is refreshed, the advertisement changes!

1. To begin, ensure that the TropicalGreen solution contains a Visual C# Class Library project named `TropicalGreenControlLib`. Otherwise, create it.

2. The project should have the following references added:
   - ° `System.Web`
   - ° `Microsoft.ContentManagement.Publishing`

3. Add a class file to the **TropicalGreenControlLib** project. Name the class **MCMSAdRotator.cs**.

4. Add the highlighted namespaces above the namespace declaration.

```
using System;
using System.Collections.Generic;
using System.Text;

using System.ComponentModel;
using System.Web.UI;
using System.Web.UI.WebControls;
using Microsoft.ContentManagement.Publishing;

namespace TropicalGreenControlLib
{
    . . . code continues . . .
}
```

5. Next, we will inherit from the `AdRotator` class. This will jumpstart our control to have all the functionalities of the out-of-the box Ad Rotator control. We will add some component design values so that the control will be given proper tag names when developers drag and drop it from the toolbox.

```
[ToolboxData("<{0}:MCMSAdRotator runat=server></{0}:
MCMSAdRotator>")] public class MCMSAdRotator : AdRotator
{
}
```

6. We will provide a property named `AdsGalleryPath`, which will contain the path to the resource gallery that contains the images. Insert the code as shown within the class declaration.

```
public class MCMSAdRotator : AdRotator
{
    // Property to get and set the path of the
    // resource gallery that contains the Ads
    private string adsGalleryPath;

     [Bindable(true)]
     [Category("Behavior")]
     [DefaultValue("")]
     [Localizable(true)]
    public string AdsGalleryPath
    {
       get { return adsGalleryPath; }
       set { adsGalleryPath = value; }
    }
}
```

7. The advertisement to be displayed will be picked randomly from the resource gallery. The `Randomizer()` method will pick a number from 1 to the number of items in the gallery at random. Here, we will use the `Random.Next()` method to generate the random number. We could go for more sophisticated methods of generating the random number, but for now, this will suffice. Add the following code below the `AdsGalleryPath` property.

```
private int Randomiser(int max)
{
   // Generate a random number
   int index = 0;
   Random rand = new Random();
   index = rand.Next(0, max);

   return index;
}
```

8. After the Ad Rotator control loads but before the page loads, the control's `AdCreated()` event is called. Here, we will first get an instance of the resource gallery and the collection of resources that make up our advertisements. We will retrieve only images—other file formats like Office documents will be ignored. Following this, we will call the `Randomiser()` method to select the advertisement to display. Once an advertisement has been selected, we set the control's properties to show the resource, link it to the URL specified in the resource's description, and set the image's tooltip (or alternate text) to the resource's display name. Append the `OnAdCreated()` event handler to the code.

```
protected override void OnAdCreated(AdCreatedEventArgs e)
{
  // Get an instance of the resource gallery that contains the Ads
  CmsHttpContext cmsContext = CmsHttpContext.Current;
  ResourceGallery rg =
     (ResourceGallery)cmsContext.Searches.GetByPath(adsGalleryPath);

  if (rg != null)
  {
     // Get only files that are images
     ResourceCollection ads = rg.Resources;
     ads.FilterByMimeType("image", true);

     // Randomly pick one of the Ads
     int resourceIndex = Randomiser(ads.Count);
     Resource r = ads[resourceIndex];

     // Display the image
     e.ImageUrl = r.Url;
     e.NavigateUrl = r.Description;
     e.AlternateText = r.DisplayName;
  }
}
```

9. The control is complete. Save the file and compile the project.

To see the control in action, first add it to the toolbox by right-clicking anywhere within the toolbox and selecting **Choose Items**. In the **Choose Toolbox Item** dialog, click browse and select the `TropicalGreenControlLib.dll` file (usually found in the `\bin\debug\` folder of the project). Once the control has been added to the Toolbox, drag and drop the control anywhere on a web form or template file. Set the `AdsGalleryPath` property to contain the path of an existing resource gallery item, such as `/Resources/TropicalGreen/PlantCatalog`. The next time you view the page, you will see rotating advertisements.

Tip #3: Considerations for Microsoft Office SharePoint Server 2007

Web Content Management (WCM) features that are today in MCMS will be part of the upcoming Microsoft Office SharePoint Server 2007 (MOSS 2007). MOSS 2007 will provide vastly richer capabilities as well:

- SharePoint and MCMS will ship as a single product, and henceforth, there will be no more confusion between the two. Along with WCM features, you will get the full suite of SharePoint capabilities such as:
  ○ Document management
  ○ Enterprise search
  ○ Surveys and discussion boards
  ○ Lists and alerts
  ○ Built-in support for portals and web parts
- In addition, MOSS 2007 includes several new exciting features:
  ○ Wikis and blogs.
  ○ An enhanced web-authoring experience (activeX components and client installations of **Site Manager** *not* required). Includes time-saving power tools such as recycle bins and one-click rollbacks to previous versions.
  ○ All the functionality in **Site Manager** is now part of the Publishing API. For example, you can programmatically administer roles, groups, and users, and other tasks that were not possible in the current version of the PAPI.
  ○ Extensible workflow built upon Windows Workflow Foundation.
  ○ Extreme scalability. Capable of handling millions of items in a single container.

MOSS 2007 will ship with many more new and enhanced features. For a complete list, take a look at the Microsoft Office SharePoint Server 2007 Guide available for download at the 2007 Microsoft Office system preview site (`http://www.microsoft.com/office/preview/servers/sharepointserver/highlights.mspx`).

For those of us who have an existing installation of MCMS and are planning to migrate to MOSS 2007, a key point to note is that WCM applications under Office SharePoint Server 2007 will use an entirely different set of APIs from the current version of MCMS. Part of the reason for the major code overhaul is the integration of the MCMS base architecture with that of Windows SharePoint Services (version 3.0).

While the complete revamp of the Publishing API will probably mean that most of the custom code that we have written for our web sites will have to be re-coded, the good news is: there will be a one-to-one mapping of functionality for most of the current properties and methods. Details may be found in the article, *Mapping MCMS 2002 APIs to SharePoint 2007* (`http://msdn.microsoft.com/office/server/ moss/2007/migration/default.aspx?pull=/library/en-us/dnmscms02/html/ CMSVersionAPIDiffs.asp`).

In addition, Microsoft will be providing migration utilities to ease the transition. The CMS Assessment Tool scans a site and generates various reports (e.g. PAPI Usage Summary Report, PAPI Class Usage Report, etc.) that will help you gauge the amount of work required to re-code your site to be ready for MOSS 2007. The CMS Assessment tool is available for download at Microsoft's web site: `http://www. microsoft.com/downloads/details.aspx?FamilyId=360D0E83-FA70-4C24- BCD6-426CAFBCC627&displaylang=en`.

For various reasons, you may not wish to migrate to Microsoft Office SharePoint Server 2007 immediately and choose to continue building your site using MCMS 2002. If that is your intention, you can take steps today to ease your migration in the future. You could:

- Isolate code that uses the PAPI into modules.
- Use the Provider Model design pattern as far as possible.

Isolate Code that Uses the PAPI into Modules

The move to change the underlying MCMS PAPI has a huge impact on existing web applications should you plan to upgrade to MOSS 2007 in the future. Unless you have used the out-of-the box solution without any form of customization, chances are you have used the PAPI to tailor the solution to meet the requirements of your website.

All the customizations that you have done using the PAPI will have to be rewritten. While rewriting code is inevitable, you can plan the code structure in such a way that the re-coding process is made as painless as possible. A good idea would be to write modular code and isolate code that uses the PAPI as far as possible. In this way, when the time comes to upgrade the website, the code that requires rewriting will be easier to locate.

Take, for example, a fairly common scenario of a custom control that lists all pages on the site that have been modified in the last seven days. Previously, the list could be programmed to be displayed in a DataGrid. The list is retrieved from the PAPI using the `Searches.NewPostings()` method. Also, when the page loads, the list is bound directly to the DataGrid using the `DataGrid.DataBind()` method. Here's an example of how the code would probably look:

```
protected System.Web.UI.WebControls.DataGrid DataGrid1;
private void Page_Load(object sender, System.EventArgs e)
{
    // Get the current CMS Http context
    CmsHttpContext cmsContext = CmsHttpContext.Current;

    // Get a list of all postings that have been modified in the last
    // 7 days
    PostingCollection newPostings = cmsContext.Searches.NewPostings(7);

    // Bind the result to the DataGrid
    DataGrid1.DataSource = newPostings;
    DataGrid1.DataBind();
}
```

To modularize the code and isolate the parts that interact with the MCMS PAPI and the parts that work with the PAPI, you could create a data abstraction layer. The data abstraction layer could be a separate class file. Before we begin modularizing the code, let's identify the parts that make use of the MCMS PAPI. The lines of code that use the PAPI are the parts that get the current CmsHttpContext and the list of postings modified in the last seven days as highlighted here:

```
protected System.Web.UI.WebControls.DataGrid DataGrid1;
private void Page_Load(object sender, System.EventArgs e)
{
    // Get the current CMS Http context
    CmsHttpContext cmsContext = CmsHttpContext.Current;

    // Get a list of all postings that have been modified in the last
    // 7 days
    PostingCollection newPostings = cmsContext.Searches.NewPostings(7);

    // Bind the result to the DataGrid
    DataGrid1.DataSource = newPostings;
    DataGrid1.DataBind();
}
```

To isolate the code, we will extract all highlighted portions of the code and add them to the data abstraction layer. In this example, the data abstraction later will simply be a separate class file called DataAbstractionExample. Here, we have two methods: GetCurrentCMSContext() gets the current CmsHttpContext, and GetListOfPostings() returns a list of all postings modified in the last seven days.

```
public class DataAbstractionExample
{
    private static CmsHttpContext GetCurrentCMSContext()
    {
```

```
        return CmsHttpContext.Current;
    }

    public static PostingCollection GetListOfPostings()
    {
        // Get the current CMS Http Contexst
        CmsHttpContext cmsContext = GetCurrentCMSContext();

        // Get a list of all postings that have been modified in the
        // last 7 days
        PostingCollection newPostings =
                        cmsContext.Searches.NewPostings(7);

        return newPostings;
    }
}
```

Next, we modify the original code to call GetListOfPostings() from the data abstraction layer instead. Notice that we have removed all code that uses the MCMS PAPI from the Page_Load() event handler.

```
protected System.Web.UI.WebControls.DataGrid DataGrid1;
private void Page_Load(object sender, System.EventArgs e)
{
    // Bind the result to the DataGrid
    DataGrid1.DataSource = DataAbstractionExample.GetListOfPostings(7);
    DataGrid1.DataBind();
}
```

At first glance, extracting all code that interfaces with the PAPI may not appear to make any difference to the behavior of the site. In fact, what we have done is added more lines of code to the application and made it a little more complex.

Nevertheless, separating the code into modular layers makes the migration process, should you choose to embark on one later, easier. Instead of making code modifications in scattered areas of the website, you could concentrate your effort on the data abstraction layers. In this example, we would only need to amend the DataAbstractionExample class, leaving the original web form (and all other web forms that use the GetListOfPostings() method) intact.

In addition, depending on your site's setup, it may be possible to run MCMS and MOSS 2007 side by side and upgrade the site in phases. In this way, you could plan to rewrite the data abstraction layers in sections. The advantage of a phased approach would mean that you get to enjoy the new features of MOSS 2007 without waiting for the entire site to be upgraded.

Use the Provider Model Design Pattern

In this book, we have discussed how the Provider Model can be used when building site navigation controls (Chapter 4) or when performing Forms Authentication (Chapter 6).

Using the Provider Model extends the idea of isolating code that uses the PAPI from other sections of code. As we have seen in earlier chapters, the Provider Model allows us to separate the "business logic", which interrogates the MCMS repository, from the "presentation logic", which is responsible for returning HTML to the browser. For example, when building the site navigation, we used the standard `SiteMapPath` and `TreeView` controls for the presentation logic. We then implemented the business logic by building the `MCMSSiteMapProvider` class, which used the PAPI to query the repository for a list of navigation items.

When it's time to upgrade the site, only the Provider Model needs to be replaced, either with native MOSS 2007 functionality or an alternative provider that speaks to MOSS. For example, to upgrade the navigation controls for the TropicalGreen site, we would just rewrite the `MCMSSiteMapProvider.cs` class file. The `SiteMapPath` or `TreeView` controls that are part of the presentation layer can be reused without further modifications.

 More details on how to plan for the future release of MOSS 2007 are available in the following white paper: http://msdn.microsoft.com/library/en-us/ dnmscms02/html/CMSDesigningCMS2002Sol.asp.

Summary

In this chapter we discussed a couple of tips that will ease developing websites with MCMS. First we saw how the `PostBackUrl` property can be used to pass data from one page to another. Following that, we devised a workaround to get it to work correctly on MCMS sites.

Next, we discussed the nifty Ad Rotator control that ships with ASP.NET 2.0. While the Ad Rotator control has been around for a while, this latest version allows us to bind the control's contents directly with a non-static XML file. We are now able to integrate the control directly with MCMS resource-gallery items, providing a flexible and useful addition to our toolbox.

Finally, we discussed some considerations for future plans to ease the migration of existing applications to the next release of MOSS 2007.

Index

MCMS sample website 91
menu control, adding 127, 128
navigation structure 106
site deployment object file, importing 92
skin, creating 155
style sheet, creating 156, 157
theme, creating 150

U

URL in link tags, correcting 161, 164

V

Virtual Directory. *See* **CMS Virtual Directory**
Visual Studio 2005
  installing 10, 11, 12, 13, 49, 52
Visual Web Developer
  MCMS application, creating 67

W

web applications
  developing 165

Advanced Microsoft Content Management Server Development

ISBN: 1904811531   Paperback: 512 pages

This book has the most in depth-coverage of important MCMS development topics found anywhere. Each author of the book is a renowned expert in the area.

1. Learn directly from recognized community experts

2. Extensive coverage of the Publishing API (PAPI)

3. Get Sharepoint and MCMS working together

4. InfoPath, RSS and hot topics covered

Windows Small Business Server SBS 2003: A Clear and Concise Administrator's Reference and How-To

ISBN: 1904811493   Paperback: 494 pages

Quickly find the information you need to install, configure and maintain all the features of SBS 2003 to get the job done.

1. Comprehensive coverage

2. Structured for speed. Find it, do it, finish

3. Perfect companion to the MS Docs and KB

Please check **www.PacktPub.com** for information on our titles